THE INVISIBLE COOK

BOOKS BY RUTH MELLINKOFF

Cookbooks

Published by the Ward Ritchie Press:
The Something Special Cookbook
The Uncommon Cookbook
The Just Delicious Cookbook

Published by Warner Books:
The Easy, Easier, Easiest Cookbook

Scholarly Books

Published by the University of California Press:
The Horned Moses in Medieval Art and Thought
The Mark of Cain

THE INVISIBLE COOK
BY RUTH MELLINKOFF

A Book of Recipes:
Carefree/Fail-Safe/Elegant

Pangloss Press
JOSEPH SIMON / PUBLISHER

Cover Serigraph by Rachelle Dubin Simon
Book Design by Joseph Simon

Library of Congress Cataloging in Publication Data
Copyright © 1983 by Ruth Mellinkoff

Mellinkoff, Ruth.
    The Invisible Cook

    Includes index.
    1. Cookery.   I. Title.
TX715.M5138   1984   001.64   83–22125
ISBN 0–934710–08–2

Preface

The philosophy behind *The Invisible Cook* is commonplace: Cook when no one is looking! But while the theory is simple, its practical application requires imagination and bold experimentation. Developing new and better ways of preparing exquisite food, but without last-minute chaos in the kitchen, has been my concern over the last 25 years. As my scholarly work has become more engrossing and demanding, my desire to discover new ways, or uncover forgotten old ones, of producing superb cuisine on my own terms has increased. On my own terms has meant: cooking as far ahead as possible; cooking when the time suits me best; storing the treasures safely; and making the delicious creations appear effortless. Working toward those goals, I have gradually become an almost invisible cook.

The successful results of those culinary experiments over the many years produced four earlier cookbooks; this is a fifth episode—new recipes reflecting my continued striving toward invisible cookery. The recipes mirror that philosophy, but in a most practical way. Clarity of instruction is emphasized and ahead-of-time procedures are included as part of each recipe. And I want to emphasize that the recipes are real: *they have not been collected, they have been cooked.*

A marvelous aura of tour-de-force magic surrounds invisible cookery, but equally important is the release from anxiety in the kitchen that it makes possible. We can then charm and entertain our guests; we can match pleasant hours in the kitchen with even more exciting ones at table with our friends.

Important instructions for using this book:

1 Recipes have been grouped together under simple chapter headings that do not describe all their possibilities. Browse through the recipes and note that many salads could serve as a fine first course, some first courses could serve as a luncheon or supper dish, and several fish dishes would make splendid first courses.

2 The number of people a recipe will serve is meant only as a guide, for that depends on the taste and appetite of guests and on the rest of the menu. Use your judgment and common sense in deciding how much to prepare.

3 All measurements are level ones unless otherwise stated.

4 Herbs listed in the ingredients are dried unless otherwise indicated.

5 "Chicken breast" means 1 side of a chicken—that is, "8 chicken breasts" would require a total of 4 whole breasts.

6 Unless otherwise specified, "flour" means white all-purpose flour.

7 Freezing procedures are included only if freezing is appropriate.

CONVERSION TABLE FOR FOREIGN EQUIVALENTS

LIQUID INGREDIENTS

Liquid Ounces	Milliliters	Milliliters	Liquid Ounces
1	29.573	1	0.034
2	59.15	2	0.07
3	88.72	3	0.10
4	118.30	4	0.14
5	147.87	5	0.17
6	177.44	6	0.20
7	207.02	7	0.24
8	236.59	8	0.27
9	266.16	9	0.30
10	295.73	10	0.33

Quarts	Liters	Liters	Quarts
1	0.046	1	1.057
2	1.89	2	2.11
3	2.84	3	3.17
4	3.79	4	4.23
5	4.73	5	5.28
6	5.68	6	6.34
7	6.62	7	7.40
8	7.57	8	8.45
9	8.52	9	9.51
10	9.47	10	10.57

Gallons	Liters	Liters	Gallons
1	3.785	1	0.264
2	7.57	2	0.53
3	11.36	3	0.79
4	15.14	4	1.06
5	18.93	5	1.32
6	22.71	6	1.59
7	26.50	7	1.85
8	30.28	8	2.11
9	34.07	9	2.38
10	37.86	10	2.74

CONVERSION TABLE FOR FOREIGN EQUIVALENTS

DRY INGREDIENTS

Ounces	Grams	Grams	Ounces
1	28.35	1	0.035
2	56.70	2	0.07
3	85.05	3	0.11
4	113.40	4	0.14
5	141.75	5	0.18
6	170.10	6	0.21
7	198.45	7	0.25
8	226.80	8	0.28
9	255.15	9	0.32
10	283.50	10	0.35
11	311.85	11	0.39
12	340.20	12	0.42
13	368.55	13	0.46
14	396.90	14	0.49
15	425.25	15	0.53
16	453.60	16	0.57

Pounds	Kilograms	Kilograms	Pounds
1	0.454	1	2.205
2	0.91	2	4.41
3	1.36	3	6.61
4	1.81	4	8.82
5	2.27	5	11.02
6	2.72	6	13.23
7	3.18	7	15.43
8	3.63	8	17.64
9	4.08	9	19.84
10	4.54	10	22.05
11	4.99	11	24.26
12	5.44	12	26.46
13	5.90	13	28.67
14	6.35	14	30.87
15	6.81	15	33.08

Contents

Appetizers and First Courses / 1

Fish and Seafood / 29

Poultry / 61

Meat / 87

Special Entrées / 105

Vegetables / 123

Salads and Salad Dressings / 139

Breads, Rolls, and Coffeecakes / 155

Cakes, Cookies, and Pastries / 171

Desserts / 213

Index / 251

Appetizers and First Courses

Alsatian Onion Pie

(serves 8 to 10 as a first course)

1 1/2 recipes of *rich pastry* (page 210)

for filling

    8 cups sliced onions
    1/4 pound butter (1 stick)
    2 teaspoons salt
    1/4 teaspoon pepper
    1 tablespoon flour
    4 extra-large eggs
    1 cup heavy whipping cream
    1/4 cup grated parmesan cheese

Preparing the pastry: Roll pastry to fit either a 10-inch quiche dish (2 inches deep) or a 12-inch quiche dish (1 1/2 inches deep). Line with greased foil and fill with beans or rice to weigh down the foil. Bake in a preheated 425° oven for 15 minutes. Remove foil and beans, reduce oven to 375°, and bake pastry shell 10 additional minutes. Remove from oven and cool.

Making the filling: Sauté onions slowly in butter, stirring frequently, until tender and golden but not brown; this usually takes 15 to 20 minutes. Sprinkle with salt, pepper, and flour, then simmer, stirring occasionally, another 2 minutes. Remove from heat and set aside until needed. Shortly before baking, preheat oven to 450°. Beat eggs and cream together, stir in cheese, and pour over onions; combine thoroughly. Pour filling into prepared pastry shell, place in oven, and then *immediately* reduce heat to 350°. Bake about 55 minutes; top should be well browned. Serve hot or warm.

To prepare ahead of time: Pastry shell can be baked 2 days ahead and stored, well wrapped, in the refrigerator. Onion mixture can be done 2 days ahead, covered and refrigerated; bring to room temperature before using. Finish by combining eggs, cream, and cheese with the onion mixture; bake as directed. The pastry shell can be frozen baked or unbaked.

Shrimp and Sole Mousse in Cabbage with Shallot Butter

(*serves 10 as a first course*)

1 pound medium-size raw shrimp in the shell
1 large cabbage
Saran wrap (do not try to use any other brand)

for sole mousse

    1 1/4 pounds fillet of sole
    2 teaspoons salt
    1/4 teaspoon white pepper
    4 egg whites
    1 1/2 cups heavy whipping cream

for shallot butter sauce

    1/2 cup heavy whipping cream
    2 tablespoons finely chopped shallots
    1/4 teaspoon salt
    1/2 pound butter (2 sticks), cut in 1-inch pieces
    1 tablespoon lemon juice

for garnish
    chopped parsley or pimento or caviar

Peel shrimp, discard shells, and refrigerate the shrimp. Remove core of the cabbage, then blanch cabbage in a large pot of salted, boiling water, gradually removing cabbage leaves as they become limp. Drain leaves and dry them carefully on towels.

Preparing the mousse: Cut fillets of sole into small pieces and place them in a food processor with the salt and pepper. Purée the sole, gradually adding egg whites, occasionally mixing carefully with a spatula. Gradually add cream and continue to process until smooth. Chill.

To assemble: Trim cabbage leaves of any hard core or too thick parts. Place each leaf on a piece of Saran wrap that is 12 by 12 inches. Place a generous tablespoon of sole mousse in center and top with 2 or 3 of the peeled shrimp. Bring cabbage leaves over the shrimp and mousse, and then wrap tightly in the Saran wrap, twisting wrap as needed to secure. Place on a tray with sealed sides down and refrigerate.

To cook: Remove cabbage rolls 1 hour before time to cook. Preheat oven to 350°. Place rolls, still in their Saran wrap, on a rack in a large roasting pan. Pour boiling water into bottom of pan (water should not touch rolls), cover pan tightly with heavy-duty foil, and place in oven to steam for 25 minutes. While cabbage rolls are steaming, make sauce.

Making the shallot butter sauce: Heat cream, shallots, and salt together until boiling, then reduce heat and simmer 1 minute. Gradually whisk in the butter and lemon juice, keeping heat on low.

To serve: Remove cabbage rolls from oven and remove Saran wrap from each. Drain quickly on paper towels and then place on very hot serving plates. Spoon some of the shallot butter sauce over each, and ganish each top with freshly chopped parsley, or a bit of pimento, or 1/2 teaspoon caviar.

To prepare ahead of time: The cabbage rolls can be assembled and refrigerated 1 day before; when ready to proceed, follow directions in recipe. Ingredients for shallot sauce should be measured and arranged near the stove ahead of time—even as early as the morning of the party. Preparing the sauce is then a quick and simple procedure.

Rumaki with Watermelon Pickles

>   fresh chicken livers, cut in halves
>   waterchestnuts, cut in thirds
>   soy sauce
>   bacon slices, cut in halves
>   watermelon-rind pickles, cut in halves

Dip liver pieces in soy sauce, then join each to a piece of waterchestnut, and wrap in half a slice of bacon. Fasten with toothpicks. Place them on a broiler rack and bake in a preheated 400° oven until bacon is cooked, about 15 minutes. Remove from oven and, as soon as cool enough to handle, remove picks and skewer each on a 5-inch bamboo pick, adding half of a watermelon pickle on each skewer. Cover lightly, leave at room temperature, and shortly before serving, return to a 400° oven for a few minutes—just until hot; serve at once.

To prepare ahead of time: Easily done in the morning; to heat, follow directions above.

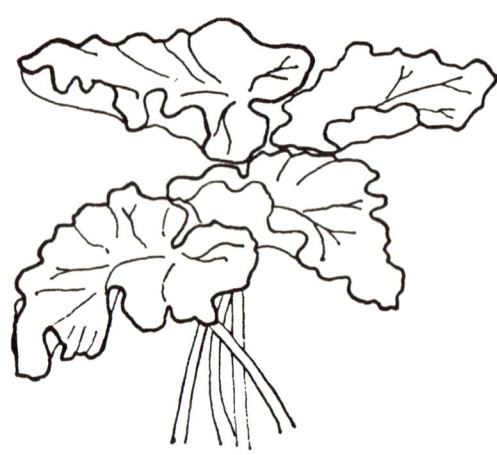

Wing-Drumsticks with Sesame Seeds

(*serves 10*)

10 chicken wings
salt and pepper
flour
2 eggs, beaten with 1 tablespoon water
2 cups sesame seeds
vegetable oil or shortening

Cut tips off chicken wings, then cut wings in half. Make 2 drumsticks from each wing, removing 1 of the little bones in the flat wing portion. Push flesh of each down to form mini-drumsticks. If boning the flat part of each wing seems too difficult, buy 20 wings instead of 10 and just use the drumstick portion.

Season wing-drumsticks generously with salt and pepper. Roll each in flour and shake off excess. Dip each in beaten egg, then roll in sesame seeds, coating them completely. Heat enough oil to form a 1/2-inch layer in a large skillet. Place wing-drumsticks in hot oil, taking care not to crowd them; cover skillet, and cook until browned on one side. (Heat should remain moderately high.) Remove cover, turn wing-drumsticks over, and continue cooking, this time without a cover, until brown. Drain on paper towels, sprinkle with more salt to your taste, and arrange in a heat-proof casserole or serving dish. Cover lightly with waxed paper. When almost ready to serve, heat wing-drumsticks, uncovered, in a preheated 400° oven for 8 to 10 minutes.

To prepare ahead of time: These can be prepared in the morning; leave them at room temperature covered with waxed paper. Shortly before serving, heat as directed above.

Fresh Asparagus in Puff Pastry

(*serves 6*)

24 fresh asparagus, peeled and cut to 5-inch lengths measured from the tips; use bottom part of asparagus stalks for another purpose
1 pound *puff pastry* (page 211)
1 egg beaten slightly with 1 tablespoon water (for egg wash)

for sauce

    1/2 cup heavy whipping cream
    4 tablespoons lemon juice
    1/4 teaspoon salt
    1/8 teaspoon pepper
    1/2 teaspoon freshly chopped tarragon (or a pinch of dried)
    1 tablespoon chopped parsley
    1/2 pound butter (2 sticks), room temperature

Preparing the pastries: Roll puff pastry to a 1/4-inch thickness, then cut into rectangles about 2 1/2 by 4 inches. Place them on a baking sheet; chill at least 30 minutes. Score the tops of the pastries lightly with a fork and brush only their tops with the prepared egg wash. *Be careful to avoid dripping egg on edges of pastry.* Chill again for at least 15 minutes, then bake in a preheated 425° oven for 10 minutes. Reduce heat to 375° and continue to bake—about another 10 minutes—until well browned. Remove from oven, cut each pastry in half horizontally, and gently remove any soft, uncooked dough. Replace tops and leave them at room temperature, covered lightly with plastic wrap.

Preparing the asparagus: Cook asparagus, uncovered, in a pot of boiling, salted water—just until barely done. The asparagus should remain a little crisp. Remove from heat, drain off most of the water, then add ice water to stop the cooking. Drain asparagus, and carefully place the stalks on layers of paper towels to absorb excess moisture. When cool and well drained, place asparagus in a glass or stainless steel pan, cover with plastic wrap, and keep refrigerated until about 4 hours before serving. Asparagus should be at room temperature so it can be reheated in the shortest possible time.

To assemble and serve: Arrange ingredients for the sauce at the stove. Reheat pastries, uncovered, in a preheated 250° oven. Reheat asparagus, covered lightly with foil, also in a 250° oven.

While they are heating, make the sauce. Bring cream to a boil, add lemon juice, salt, pepper, and tarragon, and reduce heat to very low; whisk in the butter and parsley. Remove from heat. Place the bottoms of the pastries on warm plates, top each with 4 asparagus, then spoon on 3 or 4 tablespoons of sauce, and cover with pastry tops. Serve at once.

To prepare ahead of time: Puff pastry can be prepared several days ahead of time; keep it carefully wrapped in the refrigerator. The asparagus can be cooked the day before or in the morning; keep refrigerated until about 4 hours before serving.

To freeze: Puff pastry freezes beautifully. It can be frozen as a whole piece or rolled out, cut into rectangles, and then frozen. If puff pastry is frozen whole, defrost it overnight in the refrigerator. Individual pieces will need only 5 minutes defrosting at room temperature.

Mushroom-Phyllo Hot Pastries

(*makes 4 to 6 dozen*)

1 pound phyllo
1 pound butter, melted (best if *clarified*, page 28)

for mushroom filling

    1/4 pound butter (1 stick)
    1 large onion, finely chopped
    1 pound fresh mushrooms, finely chopped
    3/4 teaspoon thyme
    1 teaspoon salt
    1/2 teaspoon pepper
    6 tablespoons flour
    2 cups sour cream

Making the mushroom filling: Melt butter and sauté the chopped onion until lightly browned. Add mushrooms, thyme, salt, and pepper, and cook for 5 or 6 minutes, stirring frequently. Sprinkle with flour and stir. Reduce heat and add sour cream, then stir constantly until mixture has thickened. Cool, then chill.

Making the appetizers: Brush 1 sheet of phyllo with butter, then divide it into 4 rectangles. (Cover remaining phyllo, first with waxed paper and then with a damp towel, to prevent drying and crumbling.) Place a rounded teaspoonful of mushroom filling on the bottom end of each piece about 1 inch inside of edges. Fold edges of phyllo over filling and roll up, brushing phyllo with butter as you roll. Repeat process with remaining phyllo. Place on greased pans and keep chilled until about 1/2 hour before serving. Bake in a preheated 400° oven until well browned—about 15 to 20 minutes, longer if cold.

To prepare ahead of time: These can be prepared 1 day ahead; keep refrigerated. To serve, bake directly from the refrigerator. They freeze well, too. Freeze before baking and defrost them only 15 minutes, then bake as directed, but for about 30 minutes.

Fresh mushroom tartlets

(*serves 8*)

8 prebaked, 4-inch tartlet shells (*rich pastry*, page 210)
1 onion, chopped
3/4 pound fresh mushrooms, sliced
6 tablespoons butter
1/8 teaspoon thyme
salt and pepper to taste
2 tablespoons flour
1 cup heavy whipping cream
8 teaspoons grated parmesan cheese

Sauté chopped onion in the butter until golden, then add mushrooms and sauté until mushrooms are barely cooked—1 or 2 minutes. Season with salt, pepper, and thyme; sprinkle with flour and stir. Remove from heat for 1 minute, then add cream, stir, and return to heat. Continue stirring until mixture begins to simmer. Cook gently for 1 minute, then remove from heat. Taste and correct seasoning.

To serve: Spoon mushrooms into shells, sprinkle top of each with 1 teaspoon grated parmesan, and place in a preheated 400° oven for 4 or 5 minutes, until hot. If desired the tops can be browned under a broiling unit.

To prepare ahead of time: Pastry shells and mushroom mixture can be made 1 day ahead. Shortly before serving, gently reheat mushroom mixture over low heat, stirring; freshen tartlet shells in a low oven. Both the tartlet shells and the mushroom mixture can be frozen; defrost, then proceed with reheating and filling shells as directed.

BIG PARTY ANTIPASTO

(serves 40 to 50)

2 cups (1-inch pieces) raw carrots
4 cups (1-inch pieces) celery
4 green peppers, cut in 1-inch pieces
2 medium-size cauliflowers, divided into flowerets
2 pounds fresh mushrooms, cut in halves or quarters
1 1/2 cups oil-cured black olives
1 1/2 cups pitted black olives
1 1/2 cups pickled cocktail onions
2 cups pimento-stuffed green olives
8 ounces canned pimento, drained and cut in pieces
32 ounces (or more) tunafish canned in oil, drained

for sauce

    2 cups cider vinegar
    2 cups salad oil (NOT olive oil)
    22 ounces ketchup (preferably Heinz)
    12 ounces chili sauce (preferably Heinz)
    1 (6-ounce) can tomato paste
    1 cup water
    1 tablespoon salt
    1/2 teaspoon black pepper
    2 tablespoons sugar
    2 (2-ounce) cans flat anchovies, drained
    dash Tabasco sauce

Combine all sauce ingredients in a very large pot—preferably stainless steel. Bring to a boil, then simmer gently for 8 to 10 minutes. Add carrots and bring to a gentle boil, then simmer for 5 minutes. Add celery, green peppers, and cauliflowerets, and cook gently for 5 minutes. Add mushrooms and oil-cured olives and cook for 5 minutes. Add pitted black olives, cocktail onions, green olives, and pimento, and cook gently a final 5 minutes. Remove from heat. Break or cut tunafish into large pieces, then add to mixture. Stir well but gently. Cover and chill at least 24 hours before serving. Store in glass or enamel containers with tight-fitting covers.

To prepare ahead of time: This should be made at least 1 day ahead. Without the tunafish, the mixture will keep 4 to 6 weeks in the refrigerator. If you plan to serve the entire amount in the recipe, add the tunafish 1 or 2 days before serving; or, if using a small amount, just add tunafish in any desired quantity, stir and serve.

Salmon and sole pâté

(*serves about 12*)

    1 pound fresh salmon fillets (all bones removed; use tweezers if necessary)
    1 1/4 pounds fresh sole fillets
    2 1/4 teaspoons salt
    1/4 to 1/2 teaspoon white pepper
    2 cups heavy whipping cream
    2 egg whites
    2 whole eggs
    green mayonnaise (page 154)

Preparing sole mousse: Cut sole fillets in pieces, then whirl in a food processor for 1 minute or less. Add salt, pepper, cream, egg whites, and whole eggs, and process until puréed.

Cut salmon in 1/2-inch wide strips (1/4- to 1/3-inch thick). Butter a 1 1/2 quart terrine or casserole and cover bottom with a layer of salmon strips. Season salmon lightly with salt and pepper. Top strips with a layer of mousse, then with salmon strips and a little more salt and pepper. Continue layering, ending with mousse on top. Cover dish tightly with buttered foil and place in a baking pan. Pour boiling water into pan to a level 1/3 the way up the sides of the terrine. Bake at 350° for about 1 hour. Cool (covered) on a rack. When mousse is at room temperature, remove foil, cover with plastic wrap, then with more foil. Chill at least 12 hours. Serve with green mayonnaise and melba toast.

To prepare ahead of time: This is best prepared at least 1 day ahead, but it can be made 3 days before. Keep tightly covered and refrigerated.

Herring with Apple, Onion, and Dill

(*serves 6 to 8*)

12 ounces wine herring snacks
1 large onion, thinly sliced
1 1/2 cups diced peeled apples
1 cup sour cream
1/2 teaspoon salt
1 or 2 teaspoons lemon juice
2 teaspoons chopped fresh dill

Drain herring and discard liquid, spices, and onion. Cut herring into bite-size (small) pieces. Place sliced onion in a bowl. Cover with boiling water and let stand for 3 minutes, then drain. Spread onion slices on paper towels to remove excess moisture. Combine onion and herring, then add remaining ingredients and mix together gently. Cover and chill.

To prepare ahead of time: This can be prepared 2 days ahead; keep covered and refrigerated. Stir again just before serving.

Pimento-Anchovy Canapés

canned pimento
canned anchovies rolled with capers
white bread, sliced
soft butter

Cut pimento into pieces about 3/4 inch in size. Drain rolled anchovies. Cut bread slices into 1 1/2-inch rounds and butter them generously. Place a pimento piece on buttered rounds, then top each with a rolled anchovy. Cover with plastic wrap until time to serve.

To prepare ahead of time: These can be prepared 1 day ahead; cover tightly and keep refrigerated. Bring to room temperature before serving. They can be prepared in the morning; leave at room temperature. In either case, keep covered until time to serve.

Chicken Liver Mousse Super Simple

(*serves 12 to 16*)

1 pound chicken livers
1 cup rich chicken stock
1/2 large onion, coarsely chopped
1 pound butter, cut in 1/2-inch slices
1 teaspoon salt
3/4 teaspoon white pepper
1 tablespoon cognac
2 tablespoons port

Place chicken livers and onion in a saucepan and cover with chicken stock. Bring to a boil, then immediately reduce heat and simmer for 12 minutes. Remove from heat and drain livers; discard chicken stock. Place livers in a food processor and purée, scraping sides of container a few times. Gradually add remaining ingredients and blend until mixture is very smooth. Place in a bowl and chill over ice, stirring occasionally, until mixture thickens and looks like creamed butter, then spoon into either 1 large terrine or individual small ones. Chill.

To prepare ahead of time: This can be prepared 2 days ahead; keep covered and refrigerated. It freezes perfectly; defrost overnight in the refrigerator.

Chicken Liver Pâté with Port Wine Aspic

(*serves 12 to 16*)

1 pound chicken livers
4 egg yolks
2 teaspoons salt
1/4 teaspoon white pepper
pinch of nutmeg
pinch of ginger
tiny pinch of cloves
1/2 pound butter (2 sticks), melted and cooled
4 tablespoons port
1 cup *crème fraîche* (page 28) or heavy whipping cream

for port wine aspic

> 1 tablespoon unflavored gelatin (1 package)
> 1/2 cup cold water
> 1/2 cup clear chicken stock
> 1 cup port
> 1 tablespoon red wine vinegar

Making the pâté: Purée livers in a food processor, then add egg yolks, port, salt, pepper, and other spices and blend. Add melted butter and whirl again. Remove to a bowl and whisk in the crème fraîche (or whipping cream). Divide mixture into very small casseroles (1/2-cup size or smaller) and arrange them in a large baking pan. Add hot water to baking pan until it reaches halfway up the sides of the small casseroles. Cover pan with foil and bake in a preheated 325° oven for 45 minutes. Remove and cool (still covered) on a rack. Wrap each casserole in plastic wrap and chill before adding aspic.

Making the aspic: Soak gelatin in the cold water for 5 minutes. Heat stock to boiling and add the soaked gelatin, stirring until dissolved. Stir in port and vinegar and remove from heat. Cool aspic over ice, stirring constantly, and as soon as it begins to look syrupy, spoon a layer of it over each pâté casserole. Chill until set.

To prepare ahead of time: These can be prepared 1 or 2 days before serving. After aspic has jelled, cover each with plastic and keep refrigerated.

Avocados filled with lobster

(*serves 6*)

3 avocados
1 1/2 pounds cooked lobster, cut in cubes
2 tablespoons vegetable oil
salt and pepper to taste
2 to 3 tablespoons *vinaigrette* (page 152)
6 to 8 tablespoons *russian dressing* (page 153)
juice of 2 or 3 lemons
juice of 3 oranges

for garnish

> mayonnaise
> fresh dill sprigs

Cut avocados in half, then with a large spoon scoop out the flesh of each half in 1 rounded piece (this makes 6). Save the avocado shells. Place the scooped avocado flesh carefully in a large bowl and cover with the lemon and orange juices. Cover bowl tightly and refrigerate. Turn emptied shells upside down on a tray and refrigerate them too. Sauté cubed lobster in the oil for 1 minute or less—only long enough to heat briefly. Remove lobster to a bowl and add vinaigrette dressing, salt, and pepper. Cover and refrigerate.

To assemble: Shortly before serving, mound lobster cubes in the empty avocado shells. Spoon russian dressing on lobster and top each with the scooped out flesh, round sides up, placing them so they look like whole avocados. Decorate edges of each (using a pastry bag, if possible) with mayonnaise and decorate tops with sprigs of dill.

To prepare ahead of time: Lobster can be cooked the day before and kept refrigerated, but do the sautéing and marinating the same day you plan to serve. The avocados can be peeled and placed in the citrus juices in the morning. Keep covered and refrigerated.

Two Canapé Cakes

(serves about 16)

2 large round loaves of caraway rye bread (New York corn rye if possible); ask bakery to cut them horizontally into 1/2-inch thick slices; 8 slices of about the same circumference are needed
softened butter
parsley, pimento, etc. to garnish

for ham mixture

    3/4 pound baked ham
    1 small onion
    1/3 cup chopped sweet pickles
    Durkee's dressing
    mayonnaise
    salt and pepper to taste

for egg mixture

    6 hard-boiled eggs
    1/3 cup chopped pimento-stuffed green olives
    mayonnaise
    salt and pepper to taste

for tomato mixture

    4 tomatoes, skinned (plunge tomatoes in boiling water for 1/2 minute to make skins slip off easily)
    4 to 6 green onions, finely chopped
    salt and pepper to taste

for cream cheese mixture

    16 ounces of cream cheese
    1 or 2 tablespoons milk or cream
    garlic salt or mashed garlic and salt to taste
    pepper to taste

Preparing the ham mixture: Grind ham, onions, and sweet pickles together (or whirl in food processor). Add Durkee's dressing and mayonnaise (half and half) to moisten, and season to taste.

Preparing the egg mixture: Chop eggs and olives (can be done in food processor or by hand). Add mayonnaise, salt, and pepper to taste.

Preparing the tomato mixture: Chop skinned tomatoes and drain well, then combine with green onions, salt, and pepper.

Preparing the cheese mixture: Whip cheese with cream or milk to spreading consistency. Season with garlic salt and pepper.

To assemble and serve: Remove crusts from bread slices and butter both sides of each slice generously. Prepare each canapé cake thus: Place 1 slice on a serving plate and cover with a thick (1/2 inch at least) layer of the ham mixture. Place second bread slice on top and press firmly. Cover this with half the tomato mixture and top with third bread slice. Cover this with half the egg mixture, then top with fourth bread slice. Frost cake, top and sides, with cream cheese mixture. Garnish with chopped parsley, sliced pimento, or both. Cover completely with plastic wrap and refrigerate until time to serve. Repeat this process for the second canapé cake. Slice canapé cakes in wedges and serve on individual plates with small forks and knives.

To prepare ahead of time: This is best prepared 1 day before serving; keep covered and refrigerated.

Anna's Smoked Haddock Mousse

(*serves 10 to 12*)

1 1/2 to 1 3/4 pounds smoked haddock on the bone (finnan haddie)
1 1/2 cups mayonnaise
4 hard-boiled eggs
1/2 cup heavy whipping cream
1 tablespoon unflavored gelatin (1 package)
1/2 cup cold water
juice of half a lemon, or to taste
salt and pepper to taste

for aspic

>1 (10 1/2-ounce) can condensed consommé
>1 tablespoon unflavored gelatin (1 package)
>1/2 cup cold water
>2 to 3 teaspoons lemon juice
>3 tablespoons dry sherry

for garnish

>lemon slices
>sliced stuffed olives
>sliced radishes
>chopped parsley

Preparing the mousse: Cover smoked haddock (finnan haddie) with half water and milk, and poach gently for 10 to 15 minutes or until it is cooked. Drain, bone, and flake. Combine flaked fish, mayonnaise, and eggs, then purée in a blender or food processor; do this in 2 batches unless you have a large-size food processor. Soak gelatin in cold water for 5 minutes, then dissolve it over simmering water. Add cream to the fish mixture, stir well, then add dissolved gelatin all at once, stirring it in quickly. Add lemon juice and season to taste. Pour into an oiled 9-inch round metal cake pan and refrigerate until firm.

Preparing the aspic: Soak gelatin in cold water. Bring consommé to a boil, then reduce heat to a bare simmer and add soaked gelatin. Stir until dissolved, then remove from heat and add lemon juice and sherry. Chill only until syrupy.

To assemble and serve: Unmold haddock mousse. Cover top with a thin layer of aspic. Chill until aspic is firm. Decorate with quartered lemon slices, sliced olives, radishes, and chopped parsley. Then carefully cover with another thin layer of aspic. Chill. Serve in pie-shaped wedges accompanied by buttered melba toast.

To prepare ahead of time: The mousse can be prepared 2 days before serving, but the aspic and garnish should be added no earlier than 1 day ahead.

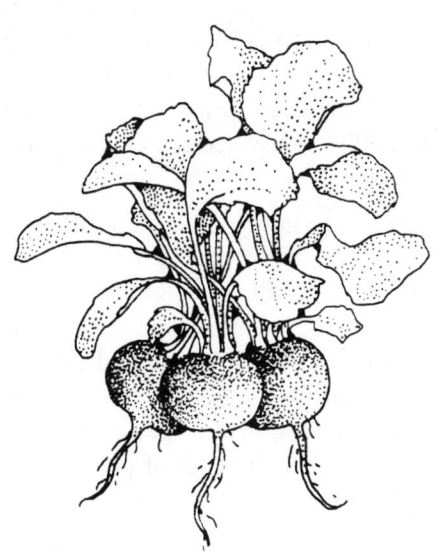

Eggs Deluxe with Caviar

(serves 10)

20 eggs
1/4 pound butter (1 stick)
salt and pepper to taste
1 cup heavy whipping cream
1 1/2 to 2 tablespoons finely chopped green onion
20 teaspoons (generous) black caviar (inexpensive lumpfish)

You will need 20 egg cups (2 for each guest) and, if possible, a special egg cutter known as a "coupe-oeuf." If you do not have the egg cutter, try cutting the eggs quickly with a razor-sharp knife. The eggs will be less perfect, but impressive and delicious nonetheless.

Slice the tops of the eggs about 1/2 inch down from their pointed ends, saving both the larger part of the shells and the little tops. Put 16 of the raw eggs in a bowl (use remaining 4 eggs for some other purpose), and remove any bits of shell. Cover bowl and refrigerate. Wash empty shells and the little caps in warm water, then drain them on paper towels. Put the larger shells in the egg cups and arrange the cups in a large baking pan (or 2 pans). Shortly before you are ready to serve, put the pan with the egg cups and shells in a preheated 225° oven to heat. This will help keep the eggs warm when it is time to serve.

To scramble and serve the eggs: Beat eggs lightly with salt and pepper. Melt butter in a large nonstick skillet over low to moderate heat. Add eggs and stir over low heat, gradually adding the cream, and cooking only until eggs have reached a scrambled but still creamy stage. Stir in the green onion and immediately remove from heat. Fill egg shells as quickly as possible and top each with a generous teaspoon of caviar. Arrange the little caps at an angle on the caviar and give 2 to each guest, if possible on a warm plate, and with a caviar or demitasse spoon.

To prepare ahead of time: The eggs can be cut in the morning; refrigerate raw eggs but leave shells at room temperature. They can also be cut the day before, but then the shells too should be refrigerated in a bowl of cold water. Rinse shells again in warm water the day you plan to serve.

Crêpe Appetizer Gâteau

(*serves 16 to 20*)

9 dinner-plate size *crêpes*, at least 10 inches in diameter (page 27)
1 1/2 pounds fresh spinach, washed and drained
1/4 cup *garlic oil* (page 28)
salt and pepper
3 cups mayonnaise
3/4 cup dijon-style mustard
1 pound thinly sliced danish ham
12 ounces thinly sliced italian salami
1 pound thinly sliced imported swiss cheese
freshly chopped parsley

Combine mayonnaise and mustard in a bowl and set aside.

Heat garlic oil in a large pot, add spinach, salt, and pepper—but no water—and sauté over moderate heat until most of the liquid has disappeared and spinach is tender. Remove from heat.

To assemble: Place 1 crêpe on a large serving dish and spread with mayonnaise-mustard. Cover with a layer of ham. Top with second crêpe and spread this with mayonnaise-mustard and cover with a layer of cooked spinach. Add third crêpe, spread with mayonnaise-mustard, and add a layer of salami. Add fourth crêpe, spread with mayonnaise-mustard, and then add a layer of sliced cheese. Now, repeat this process with 4 more crêpes. Place ninth crêpe on top of the gâteau, then cover top and sides of gâteau with remaining mayonnaise-mustard. Cover tightly with plastic wrap, and refrigerate overnight.

To serve: Remove gâteau from refrigerator 3 hours before serving. Just before serving, unwrap gâteau and sprinkle with chopped parsley. Cut in wedges and serve on individual plates with forks and knives.

To prepare ahead of time: This can be prepared 2 days ahead. Crêpes can be frozen (see page 27). Defrost them completely, then heat in their foil wrapping in a low oven, only long enough so they can be separated without tearing.

CHILES EN NOGADA

(30 portions)

30 canned whole green chiles
1/2 cup fresh pomegranate seeds

for picadillo stuffing
    2 pounds lean pork, ground twice
    2 onions, finely chopped
    1 garlic clove, mashed (or 1 teaspoon garlic from *garlic oil*, page 28)
    1 (1-pound) can whole tomatoes, chopped or mashed
    1 cup raisins, soaked in hot water, then drained
    1/4 cup dry sherry
    1/2 teaspoon cinnamon
    1/4 teaspoon powdered cloves
    salt and pepper to taste
    3/4 cup chopped almonds, lightly toasted

for cream cheese-walnut sauce
    16 ounces cream cheese
    1 cup milk
    2 cups walnuts, lightly toasted, then finely chopped or ground
    1/2 teaspoon mashed garlic (or from *garlic oil*, page 28)
    salt to taste

Preparing the stuffing: Brown pork, onion, and garlic until lightly browned. (Additional oil should not be needed.) Add tomatoes, raisins, sherry, spices, salt, and pepper. Simmer uncovered, stirring occasionally, for 15 to 20 minutes. Taste for seasoning, then add almonds and set aside.

Making the sauce: Whip cream cheese until smooth, then gradually beat in the milk. Add walnuts, garlic, and salt and mix thoroughly. Set aside at room temperature if serving the same day.

To assemble: Remove seeds from chiles; drain on paper towels. Fill each chile with a rounded tablespoon of picadillo, then roll up and place in a single layer on a large serving dish. Spoon cheese-walnut sauce on each stuffed chile and sprinkle tops with pomegranate seeds.

To prepare ahead of time: The picadillo and the cream cheese-walnut sauce can be prepared 2 days ahead and kept refrigerated; reheat the stuffing before filling the chiles and bring sauce to room temperature. Stuffing and sauce can be frozen, in separate containers; defrost completely, then proceed as directed for refrigerated filling and sauce. Pomegranates will keep for months if stored uncovered on an open shelf in the refrigerator.

TUSCAN BEAN AND TUNAFISH APPETIZER

(*serves 8 to 10*)

    1 1/2 cups dried white beans
    2 garlic cloves, mashed (or 2 teaspoons garlic from *garlic oil*, page 28)
    1 tablespoon salt
    1 onion, sliced or chopped
    1/2 to 3/4 cup fine olive oil
    3/4 teaspoon cracked black pepper
    2 (7-ounce) cans tunafish packed in oil, drained
    chopped parsley
    lemon wedges

Wash beans, then cover with water and bring to a boil. Remove from heat, but leave beans in the water for 1 hour. Drain. Add garlic to beans, and enough fresh water to cover. Bring slowly to a boil, cover and simmer 1 hour. Add salt and continue to simmer beans (covered) until tender—an additional 1/2 to 1 hour. Drain, then add onions, olive oil, pepper, and more salt if needed; mix well. Place beans in a serving dish, top with the tunafish cut into small chunks, and sprinkle with parsley. Serve chilled or at room temperature with lemon wedges.

To prepare ahead of time: The beans can be prepared and seasoned 1 week before; tunafish can be added 2 days before. Keep covered and refrigerated. Or, the beans can be cooked, seasoned, and frozen, but without the tunafish. Defrost completely, stir well, taste for seasoning, then add tunafish and serve as directed.

Avocado Fontainebleau

(serves 12)

4 avocados
4 to 6 fresh pears
lemon juice
4 cups boned, smoked whitefish
1/4 cup chopped green olives
parsley or watercress

for watercress sauce

    2 cups watercress, stems removed (about 1 large bunch)
    1/3 cup heavy whipping cream
    3/4 cup mayonnaise
    1/4 teaspoon garlic salt
    2 teaspoons lemon juice
    salt and pepper to taste
    tiny drop of green food color

for sour cream–mustard sauce

    1 1/2 cups sour cream
    3 tablespoons dijon-style mustard
    1/2 teaspoon sugar
    salt and pepper to taste

Making the watercress sauce: Whirl watercress in a blender or food processor with the other ingredients. Chill.

Making the sour cream–mustard sauce: Combine ingredients, stir, and chill.

To assemble: Peel avocados and cut in thirds. Brush with lemon juice. Peel and slice pears and dip in lemon juice. Place avocado thirds and sliced pears and some smoked whitefish on individual plates. Cover half of each with watercress sauce and the other half with sour cream–mustard sauce. Sprinkle with chopped olives and garnish with parsley or watercress.

To prepare ahead of time: The sauces can be made 2 days ahead; keep covered and refrigerated. Fish can be boned and refrigerated 1 day before and kept refrigerated. Pears and avocados can be peeled in the morning if well brushed with lemon juice, covered and refrigerated. Individual plates can be arranged an hour before serving; cover with plastic wrap.

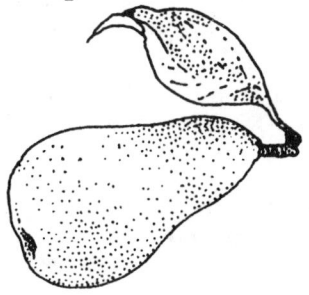

CRÊPES

(*makes about 12 7-inch crêpes*)

3 eggs
1 cup milk
3/4 cup flour
1/4 cup melted butter (1/2 stick)
1/8 teaspoon salt

Beat eggs slightly, then add flour and milk alternately. Add melted butter and salt. Let mixture stand for 1 hour or longer. Batter should have the consistency of heavy cream; add more milk if necessary. Cook crêpes in a nonstick skillet. (If you prefer, you can use any standard skillet or crêpe pan, but add a little butter to skillet before cooking each crêpe.)

To prepare ahead of time: These lend themselves to advance preparation. Stack crêpes with melted butter between each. Cool, wrap in foil (4 to 6 in a package), and either refrigerate (for 1 or 2 days) or freeze. Bring to room temperature, then reheat in their foil wrapping in a very low oven (200°) only long enough so that they can be separated and then folded or rolled without cracking or breaking.

Garlic Oil

>1 whole head of garlic (at least 10 cloves)
>salad oil (any vegetable oil except olive oil)

Put garlic cloves through a garlic press into a pint glass jar with a tight-fitting cover. Fill jar with oil, cover, and refrigerate. For recipes requiring a touch of garlic, use oil only; for a stronger flavor, increase amount of garlic by digging down in jar and lifting out some of the pressed garlic at the bottom.

To prepare ahead of time: This will keep 1 month or more, tightly covered and refrigerated.

Crème Fraîche

>1 cup heavy whipping cream
>1 cup sour cream

Combine ingredients in a bowl and stir with a whisk. Cover and leave at room temperature for 8 hours, then refrigerate overnight.

To prepare ahead of time: This will keep about 10 days if kept covered and refrigerated.

Clarified Butter

Melt 1 pound of butter (or more) slowly. Remove from heat and let it stand a few minutes, then skim off frothy top. Remove the clear, golden liquid to another container, leaving behind the milky residue. Cover and refrigerate until needed.

To prepare ahead of time: This will keep in the refrigerator 2 to 3 weeks.

To freeze: This can be frozen for 2 to 3 months.

Fish and seafood

Fresh Salmon en Papillote

(*serves 4*)

4 large pieces of nonstick parchment (about 14 by 18 inches)
3/4 cup melted butter (1 1/2 sticks)
4 large salmon steaks (3/4 to 1 inch thick)
salt and pepper to taste
4 tablespoons chopped green onion
12 thin lemon slices
fresh dill sprigs

Fold parchment pieces in half, then cut them into a half-heart shape. Open each and spoon 1 tablespoon butter on one side of each heart. Season salmon with salt and pepper, then place a salmon steak on top of buttered sides of parchment hearts. Top each with chopped green onion, lemon slices, and dill sprigs; then spoon remaining butter over each. Fold papers over and seal by folding edges together so that each fold covers another, ending with a tip that you can fasten with a metal paper clip. Place papillotes on baking pans (with sides) and refrigerate until 2 hours before baking. Place papillotes in a preheated 425° oven and bake for 12 minutes. Turn oven off and bake an additional 2 or 3 minutes. Do not overbake. Serve papillotes on large dinner plates and let guests open their own, to savor all the aroma and juices.

To prepare ahead of time: The papillotes can be assembled in the morning and kept refrigerated; remove them from the refrigerator 2 hours before baking.

SALMON WITH CHAMPAGNE SAUCE

(serves 6)

6 large salmon fillets
salt and pepper
1 cup champagne
sprig of parsley
1 cup drained canned tomatoes, chopped
3/4 pound fresh mushrooms, sliced
2 tablespoons butter
2 tablespoons flour
1/2 teaspoon freshly chopped tarragon (or 1/8 teaspoon dried)
1 cup heavy whipping cream
finely chopped parsley

Season salmon with salt and pepper and place in an oven-proof glass or stainless steel or enamel pan. Add champagne, parsley, tomatoes, and sliced mushrooms. Cover with foil and poach in a preheated 350° oven for 25 to 30 minutes. Do not overcook. Remove from oven and place salmon in another baking dish. Scatter mushrooms over fish. Cook remaining juices until reduced to 1 cup, then strain.

Melt butter, stir in flour, then add reduced fish juices and cook, stirring, until mixture comes to a boil. Add cream and simmer gently for 2 minutes. Add tarragon and season to taste with salt and pepper. Spoon sauce over fish, then place in a preheated 375° oven until hot and bubbly. Sprinkle with parsley and serve.

To prepare ahead of time: This can be prepared 1 day before, but be sure not to overcook fish. Cover wth plastic wrap and refrigerate; bring to room temperature, then heat in a 375° oven. This freezes well. Defrost 24 hours ahead in the refrigerator; bring to room temperature about 2 hours before serving, then proceed as directed.

Salmon Steaks in Foil Packets

(*serves 6*)

6 salmon steaks (1 inch thick)
lemon juice
salt and pepper
3/4 cup melted butter (1 1/2 sticks)
3 tablespoons chopped green onions
6 tablespoons grated parmesan cheese

Sprinkle salmon on both sides with lemon juice, then season with salt and pepper. Place each salmon steak on a large piece of foil and cover with butter, green onions, and parmesan. Fold and seal foil packets and place them in a large baking pan in a single layer, not touching each other. Place in a preheated 400° oven for 15 minutes; reduce heat to 350° and bake an additional 10 minutes. Serve at table in the foil packets, thus preserving aroma and all the juices, and let each guest enjoy opening his own.

To prepare ahead of time: The packets can be assembled in the morning; refrigerate, but bring to room temperature an hour or so before baking.

Sole Alma

(*serves 4*)

8 large fillets of sole
salt and pepper
1 cup *fish stock* (page 46)

for mushroom filling

    1/4 pound fresh mushrooms
    2 tablespoons butter
    1/2 onion, finely chopped
    1/8 teaspoon thyme
    1/4 teaspoon salt
    1/8 teaspoon pepper
    1 1/2 tablespoons flour
    1/2 cup sour cream

for special sauce

    2 tablespoons butter
    2 tablespoons flour
    1 1/2 cups liquid—juices from poaching sole fillets, plus milk
    2 egg yolks
    1/4 cup heavy whipping cream
    1 tomato, peeled, seeded, and chopped
    salt and pepper to taste

Making the mushroom filling: Chop mushrooms as finely as possible, with a food processor if you have one. Melt butter and sauté chopped onions until lightly browned. Add mushrooms, thyme, salt, and pepper, then cook 5 minutes or longer, stirring often, until most of the moisture has been absorbed. Sprinkle with flour, stir, and add sour cream. Cook, stirring constantly, until thickened. Remove from heat and cool.

Assembling and baking the fish: Season sole fillets with salt and pepper. Spread prepared mushroom filling on 4 of the fillets, then top them, sandwich style, with the remaining 4. Pour 1 cup of fish stock into a large shallow glass or enamel casserole. Place fish "sandwiches" in casserole, cover with foil, and poach in a preheated 400° oven for 20 to 25 minutes. Remove from oven and lift fish to another casserole or heat-proof serving platter and cover lightly while preparing sauce.

Making the special sauce: Melt butter, stir in flour, then add liquid (fish stock plus milk), and cook, stirring constantly, until it boils. Reduce heat and cook uncovered until sauce reduces and thickens. Beat egg yolks with cream in a bowl, then add hot sauce to the yolks, stirring vigorously. Return sauce to pan and cook over lowest heat, only until sauce is hot and thickens a bit more. Do not let sauce boil after egg yolks have been added. Stir in chopped tomato and taste for seasoning.

Finishing the fish: Spoon sauce over poached fish and place on the upper shelf of a preheated 400° oven until hot and lightly browned. Do not overcook! Serve at once.

To prepare ahead of time: This can be completely assembled the day before; cover with plastic wrap and refrigerate. Remove from refrigerator 2 hours before serving, then proceed with the final heating. This freezes well, too; defrost and bring to room temperature, then proceed as directed.

Sole Mousse with Sherry Sauce

(*serves 8 to 10*)

for sole mousse

> 1 1/2 pounds sole fillets
> 1/2 cup dry bread crumbs
> 2 cups heavy whipping cream
> 8 egg whites
> 2 teaspoons salt
> 1/2 teaspoon white pepper

for sherry sauce

> 4 tablespoons butter (1/2 stick)
> 3 tablespoons flour
> 1/2 garlic clove, mashed (or 1/2 teaspoon garlic from *garlic oil*, page 28)
> 2 1/2 cups light cream
> 2 tablespoons tomato paste
> 1/2 cup dry sherry

Preparing the mousse: Dice sole and purée with cream and bread crumbs in a blender or food processor. (Lacking this equipment, put fish through the finest blade of a meat grinder 4 times, then mix with bread crumbs and cream.) Put puréed fish in a large bowl and beat in salt and pepper. Beat egg whites until barely stiff, then fold into fish mixture. Spoon mixture into well-greased molds, either individual or 1 large one. Place filled molds in a pan of hot water, cover with foil, and bake in a preheated 350° oven—about 20 minutes for individual molds and about 40 minutes for a large one. Remove from oven and unmold on to a heat-proof platter. Serve with sherry sauce over each portion.

Making the sherry sauce: Melt butter, add garlic, and stir in flour. Add cream gradually and cook, stirring over low heat until mixture boils. Beat in tomato paste and simmer 2 minutes. Add sherry, simmer another minute, and remove from heat. Set aside. Reheat gently before serving.

To prepare ahead of time: Both the fish mousse and sherry sauce can be prepared 1 day ahead. Cover and refrigerate, but bring to room temperature before reheating. Shortly before serving, cover fish mousse with foil and reheat in a 300° oven—only until hot. Reheat sauce, stirring, over low heat. Sole mousse and sauce can be frozen; freeze separately. Defrost completely, then reheat as directed above.

Fish Fillets, Mexican Style

(*serves 4*)

    2 pounds fish fillets (sole, red snapper, etc.)
    salt and pepper
    1 (7-ounce) can whole green chiles, seeds removed
    1 tablespoon minced dried onion
    1 (1-pound) can tomatoes, mashed

Soak minced onion in the tomatoes and set aside. Season fish fillets with salt and pepper. Place half the chiles in a shallow casserole and top with the fish (folded in half lengthwise if fillets are thin). Cover with remaining chiles and pour tomato-onion mixture over all. Bake uncovered in a preheated 400° oven for 20 to 30 minutes, basting once or twice. (Time will depend on thickness and temperature of the fish.)

To prepare ahead of time: Chiles can be seeded in the morning and onion can be soaked in tomatoes. Casserole then takes only minutes to assemble.

Fillets of Sole Mushroomed

(*serves 6*)

12 fillets of sole
salt and pepper
3 tablespoons melted butter
1 cup dry vermouth

for sauce

>1/4 pound mushrooms, finely chopped
>4 tablespoons butter (1/2 stick)
>3 tablespoons flour
>2 cups fish stock (use stock left after poaching fish, plus milk)
>salt and pepper to taste
>freshly chopped parsley

Season fish with salt and pepper, then fold each fillet in half lengthwise. Place fish in a shallow glass or enamel casserole and cover with the butter and vermouth. Bake in a preheated 400° oven for 15 minutes, basting once. Do not overcook. Remove from oven and drain off juices to use for sauce.

Making the sauce: Sauté chopped mushrooms in the butter, stirring until lightly browned. Reduce heat, sprinkle with flour and stir. Add the stock and stir constantly until it boils, then reduce heat and simmer 5 or 6 minutes. Taste for seasoning. Place fish in a heat-proof dish or in individual casseroles and spoon sauce over the fish. Return to a 375° oven and heat until very hot, but again, do not overcook. Sprinkle with parsley and serve.

To prepare ahead of time: This can be prepared 1 day ahead up to the final heating; cover and refrigerate. Bring to room temperature about 2 hours before serving, then proceed with the final heating. This freezes well. To serve, defrost completely, then proceed with the final heating.

WHITEFISH WITH SWEET PEPPERS

(*serves about 4*)

    1 whole whitefish (3 to 4 pounds)
    1 large onion, chopped
    1/4 cup olive oil
    1 sweet green pepper, sliced
    1 sweet red pepper, sliced
    salt and pepper
    1/4 teaspoon thyme
    1 1/4 cups dry red wine
    2 tablespoons tomato paste

Sauté onion in the olive oil until lightly browned. Add peppers and sauté 2 minutes, then add 3/4 cup of the red wine, tomato paste, and seasonings. Simmer gently for 5 to 8 minutes, then remove from heat. Season fish inside and out with salt and pepper. Put some of the vegetable mixture on the bottom of a baking pan and some inside the fish. Place fish on top of vegetables and cover it with remaining vegetables. Cover pan lightly with foil and bake in a preheated 350° oven for 1 hour or a little longer, basting occasionally with the remaining red wine. Serve each guest a portion of fish with some of the vegetables and sauce spooned over the top.

To prepare ahead of time: The vegetable mixture can be prepared 1 day before; keep covered and refrigerated. Bring to room temperature before baking the fish.

Rex Sole in Red Wine with Whipped Butter Sauce

(*serves 6*)

6 large rex soles (or 12 small ones)
salt and pepper

for poaching sole

>2 cups dry red wine
>2 cups water
>2 garlic cloves, split (or 2 teaspoons of garlic from *garlic oil*, page 28)
>1 small onion, chopped
>1/2 teaspoon salt
>1/4 teaspoon pepper
>4 very large shallots, thinly sliced

for whipped butter sauce

>1 tablespoon finely chopped shallots
>1/4 cup dry white wine
>2 tablespoons white wine vinegar
>1/4 teaspoon salt
>1/8 teaspoon pepper
>3/4 pound chilled butter (3 sticks), sliced thin

Preparing the whipped butter sauce: Cook the 1 tablespoon chopped shallots, wine, vinegar, salt, and pepper together until reduced to about 1 1/2 tablespoons, then gradually whip in the sliced chilled butter (use a whisk for this). Mixture should have the texture of hollandaise sauce. Set aside until ready to use. Some say this sauce must be made at the last minute, but if you whip it again before using—either at room temperature or over barely simmering water—it can successfully be prepared in advance. Do not, however, overheat; barely warm is sufficient for the sauce if fish is hot and is served on hot plates.

Preparing the fish: Cook red wine, water, garlic, onion, salt, and pepper together uncovered for 15 minutes. Strain. Season fish with salt and pepper and place in a large shallow casserole. Pour strained wine mixture over fish and top with the sliced shallots. Poach in a preheated 400° oven for 15 minutes. Remove fish from poaching liquid and serve on hot dinner plates. Top each with some of the sliced shallots and a generous spoonful of whipped butter sauce.

To prepare ahead of time: Butter sauce can be prepared 2 days before; keep covered and refrigerated. Bring to room temperature before using, then proceed as directed. Butter sauce can be frozen; defrost and bring to room temperature before proceeding.

Whole poached fish with guacamole

(*serves 10 to 12*)

1 whole fish (7 to 8 pounds)— ling cod, salmon, or other (inside center bones removed)
cheesecloth

for court bouillon

    2 large onions, sliced
    salt and pepper
    1 bay leaf
    1/2 teaspoon thyme
    juice of 2 lemons
    2 quarts water

for guacamole

    4 large ripe avocados
    juice of 1 or 2 lemons
    dash Tabasco
    garlic salt to taste

for garnish

    sliced pimento olives
    strips of canned green chiles or green pepper

Preparing court bouillon: Combine sliced onions, salt, pepper, bay leaf, thyme, lemon juice, and water in a large saucepan and simmer for 15 to 20 minutes. Remove from heat. Season fish, wrap in cheesecloth, and place in a large roasting pan. Pour court bouillon over fish, cover roasting pan, and place in a preheated 375° oven. Bake about 1 hour, or until fish flakes easily. Remove from oven, let fish cool in broth, and if possible, chill fish in the broth in the refrigerator overnight.

To assemble: Remove fish from roasting pan and place on a large platter. Remove cheesecloth and skin carefully. Pour off accumulated moisture, soaking up with paper towels what you cannot easily drain off. Make guacamole by mashing avocados and combining with the other ingredients. Completely cover fish with a thick layer of guacamole, then decorate with sliced olives (to indicate fish scales) and strips of peppers (to indicate tail and fins). If not serving immediately, cover with plastic wrap and keep refrigerated.

To prepare ahead of time: Fish can be cooked the day before and refrigerated. Even the guacamole can be prepared a day ahead if covered tightly and refrigerated; stir well before using. Coat fish not more than 2 hours before serving. Guacamole freezes; defrost a few hours before covering fish, stir well, then cover fish as directed.

Pike Baked with Vegetables and Red Wine

(serves about 4)

1 whole pike (2 1/2 to 3 pounds)
salt and pepper
3/4 cup melted butter (1 1/2 sticks)
1 large onion, chopped
1 green pepper, chopped
1 1/2 cups chopped celery
2 large carrots, chopped
2 cups stewed tomatoes, mashed
3/4 cup dry red wine

Season pike with salt and pepper and set aside. Combine butter and chopped vegetables in a large baking pan and bake in a preheated 400° oven for 10 minutes. Remove from oven and place pike on top of vegetables; spoon some inside the fish. Add tomatoes and wine, baste, and return to oven. Bake, basting occasionally, for an additional 30 to 40 minutes. Serve hot with a spoonful of vegetables over each portion.

To prepare ahead of time: Vegetables can be chopped in the morning; refrigerate them in a plastic bag.

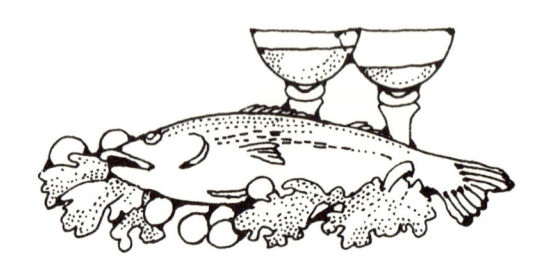

Trout Baked with Sour Cream

(*serves 4*)

    4 fresh trout (about 10 ounces each)
    salt and pepper
    lemon juice
    1 tablespoon butter
    1 tablespoon flour
    1 cup sour cream
    1/2 teaspoon salt
    1/4 teaspoon pepper
    1 green pepper, sliced
    4 to 6 green onions, chopped

Season trout with salt, pepper, and lemon juice. Place in a large buttered shallow casserole or baking pan (glass, enamel, or stainless steel). Melt butter, stir in flour, and add sour cream, stirring until it boils. Remove from heat and add salt and pepper. Divide this sauce over the trout and top each with green pepper and onion. Cover with foil and bake in a preheated 425° oven for 10 minutes. Remove foil, reduce heat to 350°, and bake 15 minutes more.

To prepare ahead of time: The pepper can be sliced and the onions chopped in the morning; cover and refrigerate. The sauce can be done in the morning, too; cover and leave at room temperature.

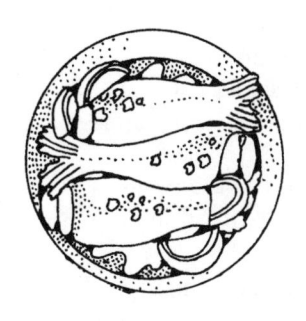

Trout Filled with Halibut Mousse
(serves 4)

4 fresh trout (inside center bones removed)
1/2 cup dry white wine
salt and pepper

for fish stock

1/2 pound fish bones, from white-fleshed fish
1 cup dry white wine
1 cup water
1/4 teaspoon thyme
1/2 teaspoon salt
1 onion, sliced

for halibut mousse

3/4 pound halibut fillets
1 teaspoon salt
1/4 teaspoon white pepper
1 1/3 cups heavy whipping cream
3 egg whites

for special sauce

2 tablespoons butter
2 tablespoons flour
1 1/2 cups strained fish stock
1/4 cup heavy whipping cream
salt and pepper to taste
2 tablespoons tomato paste
1/4 cup raisins, rinsed in hot water, then drained

Making the fish stock: Combine ingredients for fish stock and cook over moderate heat for 30 minutes, uncovered half the time. Strain and set stock aside.

Preparing the halibut mousse: Dice halibut, then whirl in a blender or food processor with cream and egg whites. Beat in salt and pepper. (Lacking this equipment, put halibut through a meat grinder 4 or 5 times, then gradually work in cream and egg whites.)

Making the special sauce: Melt butter, stir in flour, then gradually add fish stock, stirring constantly until mixture boils. Add cream, salt, pepper, and tomato paste and blend. Simmer gently, uncovered, for 5 to 10 minutes. Add raisins and simmer an additional 1 minute. Set aside.

To cook and serve: Sprinkle each trout inside and out with salt and pepper. Fill each trout very generously with halibut mousse, then place them in a buttered shallow glass or enamel pan. Pour the 1/2 cup dry white wine over the trout, cover loosely with foil, and place in a preheated 400° oven for about 25 minutes (a little longer if the fish is very cold). Remove from oven, and with the help of two large spatulas, lift each trout, drain, and place on hot serving dish or individual warm dinner plates. Serve a spoonful of the reheated special sauce over each trout.

To prepare ahead of time: Fish stock, special sauce, and halibut mousse can be prepared the day before; keep covered and refrigerated. Both fish stock and special sauce can be frozen. Defrost completely; reheat special sauce shortly before serving.

Trout "in the Manner of" La Pyramide

(serves 4)

4 medium-sized fresh trout

for fish stock

> 1 pound fish bones, from white-fleshed fish
> 2 cups dry white wine
> 2 cups water
> 1 onion, sliced
> 1 teaspoon salt

for vegetable stuffing

> 1 cup finely chopped carrots
> 3/4 cup finely chopped celery
> 5 large mushrooms, finely chopped
> 4 tablespoons butter (1/2 stick)
> 4 tablespoons flour
> salt and pepper to taste
> 4 egg yolks
> 1/2 cup heavy whipping cream

for poaching trout

> 1 carrot, chopped
> 1 onion, chopped
> salt and pepper to taste
> pinch of thyme
> 1/2 cup port
> 2 cups fish stock (see recipe above)

for sauce and garnish

    2 tablespoons butter
    2 tablespoons flour
    1 cup juices from poaching trout
    1/2 cup heavy whipping cream
    1/4 cup port
    1 teaspoon lemon juice
    2 egg yolks
    salt and pepper to taste
    12 small cooked shrimp (optional)
    12 small mushroom caps, sautéed (optional)
    parsley sprigs

Making the fish stock: Combine ingredients for fish stock in a saucepan and cook uncovered for 30 minutes. Strain.

Preparing the vegetable stuffing: Sauté the carrots in the butter in a covered skillet over low heat for 10 minutes. Add celery and mushrooms and cook an additional 5 minutes. Season to taste, sprinkle with the flour, and stir. Combine egg yolks and cream and add to the vegetables, stirring vigorously until mixture is thick. Remove from heat and cool, then chill.

Cooking the trout: Season trout with salt and pepper and stuff each with chilled vegetable stuffing. Skewer each stuffed trout closed, then place in a large shallow glass, stainless steel, or enamel roasting pan. Pour over the stuffed fish all the ingredients listed for poaching trout. Cover with foil and bake in a preheated 350° oven for approximately 25 minutes—possibly longer if stuffed trout are cold. Remove from oven and transfer fish to a heat-proof platter and remove skewers. Strain remaining juices and reserve 1 cupful to use in making sauce.

Making the sauce: Melt butter, stir in flour, then add reserved 1 cup of juices and cook over low heat, stirring constantly, until mixture comes to a boil. Add port and lemon juice. Beat egg yolks slightly with the cream, then add to sauce, beating constantly. Season to taste, and pour over the trout. Reheat briefly in a low oven if needed, then garnish each trout with 3 shrimp, 3 sautéed mushroom caps, and sprigs of parsley. [*continued on next page*]

To prepare ahead of time: This can be prepared 1 day before. Pour a little of the sauce over the cooked fish, cover and refrigerate. Remove from refrigerator 2 or 3 hours before serving, cover with foil, and place in a preheated 350° oven just long enough to become piping hot. While fish is reheating, reheat remaining sauce over low heat, stirring. Then remove fish from oven, cover with sauce, and garnish.

Trout Cornmealed

(*serves 2*)

2 small river trout
salt and pepper
lemon
1 egg, slightly beaten
cornmeal
vegetable oil
1/2 cup sliced almonds
3 tablespoons butter
lemon wedges

Rub trout with lemon, then season with salt and pepper. Dip trout into egg (or brush egg on trout) and roll in cornmeal. Sauté in hot vegetable oil until well browned on both sides, then drain on paper towels. Place trout on an oven-proof platter and keep warm in a very low oven while you sauté almonds in butter. Cook almonds only long enough to brown them lightly; be careful not to burn the butter. Pour almonds and butter over trout and serve with lemon wedges.

To prepare ahead of time: You can season trout, brush with egg, and roll in cornmeal in the morning. Place in refrigerator, uncovered, until ready to cook.

Lobster with Waterchestnuts

(*serves 4*)

2 (8-ounce) cooked lobster tails
1 (8-ounce) can waterchestnuts, drained and sliced
2 tablespoons butter
2 tablespoons sherry
grated parmesan cheese

for sauce

> 2 tablespoons butter
> 2 tablespoons flour
> 3/4 cup milk
> 1 teaspoon minced dried onion
> salt and pepper to taste
> 1 teaspoon dry mustard
> 1 teaspoon freshly chopped parsley
> 2 egg yolks, slightly beaten
> additional parsley to garnish

Preparing the sauce: Melt butter, stir in flour, and remove from heat. Add milk, minced onion, salt, pepper, and mustard, then return to heat and cook, stirring constantly, until mixture boils. Remove from heat, beat in egg yolks and parsley, then set aside.

Take lobster meat from tails and cut into large cubes. Sauté them in 2 tablespoons of butter for 1 minute, then add sherry and remove from heat. Stir in sliced waterchestnuts and the prepared sauce. Taste for seasoning.

Fill individual casseroles (or 1 large casserole) and cover tops with a generous sprinkling of grated parmesan. Place in a preheated 400° oven (on the upper shelf) and bake until hot and browned—about 15 to 20 minutes. The time will depend on how cold the lobster mixture is when you put it in the oven.

To prepare ahead of time: You can make this 1 day before, except for the final baking. Cover and refrigerate; remove from refrigerator 2 hours before baking. This freezes well. Defrost, bring to room temperature, then bake as directed.

Lobster Tails with Butter and Lemon

(*serves 4*)

2 large (1-pound) frozen lobster tails
salt and pepper to taste
1/2 cup melted butter (1 stick)
juice of 1 lemon
additional melted butter
lemon wedges

Defrost lobster tails, then split them in half lengthwise. Gently lift meat from shell, and using a small, very sharp knife, remove the thin reddish layer of skin on the shell side of the lobster meat. Place back in the shells, season with salt and pepper, and place them in a baking pan. Combine butter and lemon and spoon half of it over the lobster. Bake in a preheated 450° oven for 8 minutes, baste with remaining butter-lemon mixture, return to oven and bake an additional 6 or 7 minutes. Serve hot with more melted butter and lemon wedges on the side.

To prepare ahead of time: The lobster can be readied in the morning; cover and refrigerate. Bring to room temperature about 45 minutes before baking, then proceed with the recipe.

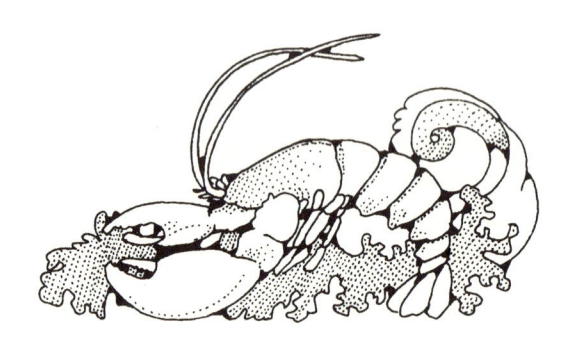

Scallops with Tomatoes and Garlic

(*serves 4 to 6*)

1 large onion, finely chopped
olive oil
1 1/2 pounds scallops (if large, quarter them)
salt and pepper
flour
2 garlic cloves, mashed (or 2 teaspoons garlic from *garlic oil*, page 28)
2/3 cup dry white wine
2 cups chopped tomatoes (fresh or canned, but not too much liquid)
4 tablespoons dry bread crumbs
2 tablespoons freshly chopped parsley

Sauté onion for 2 or 3 minutes in 1 tablespoon of olive oil. Remove from skillet. Season scallops with salt and pepper, then dust with flour, shaking off excess. Sauté scallops in 2 tablespoons of olive oil over moderate heat until lightly browned. Sprinkle with half the cooked onion, add wine, and cover. Simmer gently for 1 minute, then remove from heat—do not overcook.

In another skillet, heat 2 tablespoons of olive oil to sizzling; add tomatoes and stir vigorously. Add remaining cooked onions and garlic, then reduce heat and simmer for 1 or 2 minutes. Season with salt and pepper and simmer another minute. Place tomato mixture in the bottom of a shallow casserole. Cover with scallops, sprinkle with bread crumbs and parsley, and bake uncovered in a preheated 400° oven for about 10 minutes. Scallops should be very hot but not overcooked.

To prepare ahead of time: Scallops can be assembled the day before to the point of final heating; cover and refrigerate. Bring to room temperature about 2 hours before serving, then proceed with the baking.

Neptune's Favorite Shrimp

(*serves 6*)

3 pounds raw jumbo shrimp in shells
4 quarts water
1/3 cup salt
4 garlic cloves (or 4 teaspoons garlic from *garlic oil*, page 28)
2 large onions, sliced
juice of 2 lemons
1 cup vinegar
4 celery stalks
1/4 teaspoon thyme
1/4 teaspoon basil
2 bay leaves
sprig of parsley
1 1/2 cups fresh dill (about 1 large bunch)
few drops Tabasco

for dill-watercress sauce

>3/4 cup chopped watercress
>1/4 cup finely chopped fresh dill
>2 tablespoons chopped parsley
>1 cup mayonnaise
>1 cup sour cream
>juice of 1 lemon
>salt and pepper to taste
>garlic to taste (or use oil from *garlic oil*, page 28)

Making the dill-watercress sauce: Combine all sauce ingredients and chill several hours or longer.

Remove sand veins from shrimp but leave shrimp in their shells. Combine ingredients other than shrimp in a large pot and cook over moderate heat for 30 minutes. Strain, then return liquid to the pot. Shortly before serving, bring seasoned broth to a boil, add shrimp, bring to a gentle simmer and cook about 2 minutes—only until shrimp have turned bright pink. Do not overcook and do not let the liquid boil hard—just a simmer, or shrimp will toughen. Drain and serve at once if you plan to eat the shrimp hot. Pass the dill-watercress sauce in a separate bowl. The shrimp are equally delicious served cold.

To prepare ahead of time: The dill-watercress sauce can be made 3 days before; keep covered and refrigerated. The seasoned broth for cooking the shrimp can also be prepared 3 days before; keep covered at room temperature. If shrimp are to be served cold, cook them the day before, drain, and chill.

SHRIMP AND MUSHROOMS IN PHYLLO

(*makes about 18 rolls*)

2 pounds phyllo
1 1/2 pounds butter, melted

for filling

    1 1/2 pounds cooked peeled shrimp
    1 1/4 pounds fresh mushrooms, sliced
    1 (8-ounce) can waterchestnuts, drained and sliced
    12 ounces canned artichoke bottoms, diced
    1 onion, chopped
    12 tablespoons butter (1 1/2 sticks)
    1/2 cup flour
    2 1/2 cups milk
    1/2 cup heavy whipping cream
    1 1/2 to 2 teaspoons salt
    1/2 teaspoon pepper
    2 cups grated parmesan cheese
    1/2 cup sherry

Making the filling: Sauté onion in 6 tablespoons of butter until tender and light brown. Add mushrooms and sauté until juice has disappeared, then remove from heat. In another saucepan, melt remaining 6 tablespoons of butter and stir in flour; remove from heat. When bubbling has stopped, add milk, cream, salt, and pepper. Return to heat and cook, stirring constantly, until mixture boils. Reduce heat and cook another 2 minutes. Add cheese and stir until melted, then remove from heat and add sherry. Now add mushroom-onion mixture, shrimp, and artichoke bottoms. Cool to room temperature, then cover and chill at least 2 hours.

Making the rolls: Unroll phyllo leaves—only one package at a time—and cut them in half lengthwise. (Cover remaining phyllo, first with waxed paper and then with a damp towel, to prevent drying and crumbling.) Spread melted butter on 4 of the rectangles, then stack them 1 on top of another. At the narrow end of the stacked rectangles, place 2/3 cup of filling, leaving a 1 1/2-inch border on each side. Fold in sides and roll up jelly-roll style. Repeat process using remaining phyllo. Brush outside of each roll with more butter and place in baking pans. Chill again. Shortly before serving, bake on the lower shelf of a preheated 425° oven for 25 to 30 minutes.

To prepare ahead of time: These can be assembled the day before; cover and refrigerate. They can also be frozen. Freeze the unbaked rolls on cookie tins, then remove and wrap individually in foil and return to freezer. To serve, defrost for 2 hours, then bake for approximately 40 minutes.

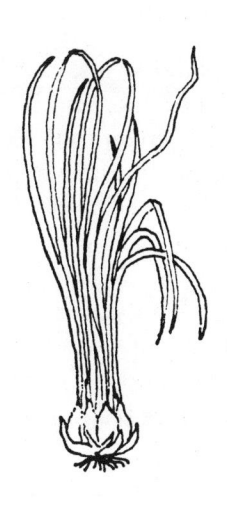

Shrimp Greek Style

(serves 4)

1 1/2 pounds extra-large raw shrimp in shells

for sauce

    1 large onion, chopped
    2 garlic cloves, mashed (or 2 teaspoons garlic from *garlic oil*, page 28)
    1/4 cup olive oil
    1 (16-ounce) can tomato purée
    1 teaspoon salt
    1/2 teaspoon pepper
    1/2 teaspoon basil
    1/2 teaspoon oregano
    4 ounces feta cheese

Preparing the sauce: Sauté garlic and onion in the olive oil for several minutes, then add tomato purée, salt, pepper, sweet basil, and oregano. Simmer for about 30 minutes, part of the time uncovered.

Open shrimp and remove sand veins, but leave shrimp in their shells. Place a large spoonful of sauce in the bottom of a casserole. Place shrimp on the sauce; cover with remaining sauce and crumble feta cheese on top. Bake, uncovered, in a preheated 350° oven for about 30 minutes—until very hot. Shrimp should be cooked in that time unless they are very cold.

To prepare ahead of time: The sauce can be prepared 5 days before; keep covered and refrigerated. Casserole can be combined the morning of your party and refrigerated; bring to room temperature about 2 hours before baking. The sauce can be frozen; defrost completely before using.

Hot seafood salad

(serves about 16)

1 pound baked ham, diced
1/4 cup butter (1/2 stick)
1 1/2 pounds fresh mushrooms, sliced
2 pounds cooked shrimp
1 1/2 pounds crab meat
2 bunches of green onions, chopped
2 1/2 cups chopped celery
2 green peppers, chopped
2 cups mayonnaise
1/3 cup lemon juice
2 teaspoons Worcestershire sauce
few dashes Tabasco
1 garlic clove, mashed (or 1 teaspoon garlic from *garlic oil*, page 28)
salt and pepper to taste

for topping

    1 cup dry bread crumbs
    1/4 cup butter
    1/4 cup grated parmesan cheese

Sauté diced ham in 1/4 cup butter for 1 or 2 minutes. Add mushrooms and cook for 5 minutes, then remove from heat. Add seafood, green onions, celery, green pepper, mayonnaise, lemon juice, Worcestershire sauce, Tabasco, garlic, salt, and pepper. Blend well and set aside.

Prepare buttered crumbs by combining the dry bread crumbs, 1/4 cup butter, and parmesan cheese in a skillet, heating slowly and stirring until crumbs are lightly browned—2 or 3 minutes.

Spoon seafood mixture into one or more casseroles, then cover with prepared crumbs. Bake in a preheated 350° oven for 15 minutes or longer—depending on how cold the mixture is.

To prepare ahead of time: This can be assembled the day before, but do not bake; cover and refrigerate. Bring to room temperature and bake as directed.

CRAB, SHRIMP, AND OYSTER GUMBO

(*serves 6*)

2 pounds baby okra
1/4 pound butter (1 stick)
2 large onions, finely chopped
2 tablespoons flour
3 cups canned tomatoes, including liquid
5 cups rich chicken broth
salt and pepper to taste
dash cayenne pepper
2 pounds raw shrimp
1 1/2 pints oysters
2 whole cooked crabs (at least 1 1/2 pounds each), well cracked

Peel and devein shrimp, then refrigerate. Chop or slice the okra, then sauté in 6 tablespoons of the butter in a heavy skillet, cooking and stirring until white strings have completely disappeared. This will take at least 15 to 20 minutes. Remove okra from skillet. Add remaining butter to skillet and sauté the onions until well browned. Sprinkle with the flour, stir, then add tomatoes and cook, stirring constantly, until mixture comes to a boil. Add chicken broth and sautéed okra, season, cover and simmer, stirring occasionally, for 2 to 3 hours. Taste for seasoning: a true gumbo should be on the peppery side.

Before serving, bring the sauce to a simmer, add the raw shrimp and cook 2 minutes. Add oysters and cook another minute. Add cracked crab and cook only until mixture comes to a gentle simmer. Do not overcook or seafood will toughen. Reheat before serving, but gently!

Serve gumbo in large soup bowls (with or without a spoonful of cooked rice).

To prepare ahead of time: Sauce for the gumbo can be made 3 days before; keep covered and refrigerated. To serve, heat sauce, then add seafood as directed in recipe. Sauce for the gumbo freezes beautifully; defrost, heat, then add seafood as instructed.

Poultry

Roasted Chicken Pomegranate

(*serves about 4*)

    1 roasting chicken (5 to 6 pounds)
    salt and pepper
    2 tablespoons sugar
    1 tablespoon cinnamon
    2 onions, chopped
    3/4 cup fresh pomegranate juice (about 2 pomegranates)
    1/4 cup dry white wine

Season chicken with salt and pepper. Mix sugar and cinnamon together, then mix with the chopped onion. Fill cavity of the chicken with some of the onion mixture; place the rest on the bottom of a heavy casserole. Place chicken on top of onions and pour pomegranate juice and wine over the chicken. Cover tightly with a heavy cover, or double wrap in heavy-duty foil. Place in a preheated 450° oven and roast without removing the cover for 1 hour and 15 to 30 minutes; time depends on the weight and temperature of the chicken. Remove chicken to a platter. Carve and serve with the juices and onions in the bottom of the casserole.

To prepare ahead of time: The chicken can be seasoned and arranged in the casserole with the onion mixture in the morning; cover and leave at room temperature. Pomegranate juice can be extracted 2 days before; keep refrigerated.

Waterzooï Chicken (My Way)

(serves about 6)

2 large frying chickens, quartered
2 large onions, sliced
1 1/2 cups sliced celery
1 1/2 cups sliced carrots
2 tablespoons butter
6 cups chicken stock
2 teaspoons salt (or to taste)
1/2 teaspoon pepper
1 bay leaf
1/4 teaspoon thyme
1/4 teaspoon nutmeg
4 egg yolks
1/4 cup heavy whipping cream
1 tablespoon lemon juice

Remove excess fat from chickens. Melt butter in a large casserole or pot, then add onions, celery, and carrots. Sauté over moderate heat, stirring frequently, for about 5 minutes—until vegetables begin to brown. Add chicken, chicken stock, and seasonings. Cover and cook over gentle heat until chicken is just tender. Do not overcook. Remove from heat and discard bay leaf. Let chicken cool in the stock to room temperature, then remove chicken pieces and discard all skin and bones.

Place chicken pieces in a bowl and spoon a little broth over them; cover with plastic wrap and set aside. Strain broth, BUT RESERVE VEGETABLES. Place broth back in pot and cook over high heat for 3 minutes. Purée vegetables in a food processor and add them to the broth. Taste for seasoning.

Shortly before serving, bring broth–vegetable mixture to a gentle simmer. Beat egg yolks and cream in a bowl; add a little of the hot broth to the yolk mixture and beat well, then add egg mixture to the hot broth, but be sure the broth is not boiling. Over lowest heat, add chicken pieces and lemon juice, and stir gently until mixture is hot, but again—watch that it does not boil. (If it does boil, it may curdle; however, it will still taste delicious though its texture is not as smooth.) Serve very hot in heated large soup bowls.

To prepare ahead of time: This can be completely prepared ahead of time and reheated if proper care is taken to reheat gently so that the mixture does not curdle. The same precaution applies should you freeze this; defrost completely, then reheat slowly and gently, stirring occasionally.

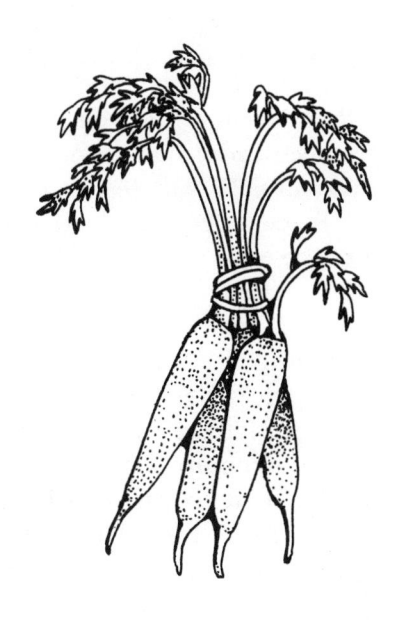

MONTE ALBAN CHICKEN EN PAPILLOTE

(*serves 8*)

8 chicken breasts, skin removed
salt and pepper
flour
1/8 pound butter (1/2 stick)

for Monte Alban sauce

    2 tablespoons butter or oil
    3 garlic cloves, mashed (or 3 teaspoons garlic from
      garlic oil, page 28)
    1 (1-pound) can tomatoes
    1 tablespoon dried oregano
    1 tablespoon ground cumin
    1/2 teaspoon salt
    1 teaspoon chili powder
    1/4 pound cold butter (1 stick), sliced

Making the sauce: Sauté the garlic and onion in the butter or oil for 3 or 4 minutes, then add the tomatoes, mashing them well. Simmer for 5 minutes, then add the oregano, cumin, salt, and chili powder. Simmer covered for 15 minutes; uncover and simmer an additional 5 minutes. Place sauce in a blender or food processor, then add cold butter slices and whirl until smooth. Set aside.

Preparing the chicken: Season chicken breasts with salt and pepper, roll in flour, then sauté in the 1/4 cup butter until browned and almost tender. Set aside. Take 8 nonstick parchment sheets, about 12 by 18 inches, and fold in half. Cut folded sheets in the shape of half a heart and open up. Place a chicken breast in the center on one side of the heart, cover with 1/4 to 1/3 cup of the sauce, then fold over and seal the edges of the parchment by folding them over and over each other; fasten ends with paperclips. Place them on a baking pan (with sides) and bake in a preheated 350° oven for approximately 20 minutes if at room temperature or longer if cold.

To prepare ahead of time: The Monte Alban sauce can be prepared 2 days ahead and papillotes can be assembled 1 day before. Refrigerate. Before serving, bake as directed. They can be frozen. Freeze papillotes before baking on a baking tin and when frozen, store in large plastic bags, tightly closed. Defrost completely, then bake as directed.

OLD-FASHIONED FRIED CHICKEN

>   chicken breasts, thighs, drumsticks
>   salt and pepper
>   flour
>   vegetable oil or shortening

Season chicken generously with salt and pepper. Roll pieces in flour and shake off excess. Heat enough oil or shortening to form a 1/2-inch layer in a heavy skillet, then place chicken in skillet skin sides down. Do not crowd the chicken pieces. Cover skillet and cook over moderately high heat until well browned on skin side. Remove cover, turn chicken so skin sides are up, and continue cooking—uncovered, now—until undersides of chicken are browned and chicken is completely cooked. Drain on paper towels, then place in a baking dish in a single layer. Cover lightly with waxed paper and leave at room temperature. Shortly before serving, place chicken in a preheated 400° oven on the upper shelf and heat uncovered 10 to 15 minutes—until very hot.

To prepare ahead of time: The chicken can be fried in the morning. Leave at room temperature, lightly covered; reheat as directed.

Mexican Chicken with Green Sauce

(*serves 8 to 10*)

3 frying chickens, quartered
salt and pepper
2 cups chicken stock
1 chicken bouillon cube
1 cup dry-roasted sunflower seeds
1 cup blanched almonds
1 (7-ounce) can whole green chiles (seeds removed)
2 (12-ounce) cans Mexican tomatillos, well drained
1 onion, coarsely chopped
1/2 cup fresh coriander (leaves only)
salt to taste
2 tablespoons oil

Place quartered chickens in a large roasting pan and season with salt and pepper. Dissolve bouillon cube in stock and pour over chicken. Cover and roast in a preheated 350° oven for 40 to 45 minutes—until almost tender. Do not overcook. Remove from oven and drain off the juices to use in making the sauce.

Making the sauce: Pulverize sunflower seeds in a blender or food processor, then pulverize almonds and combine with sunflower seeds. Purée the chiles, tomatillos, onion, and coriander in the blender (or food processor) and combine with ground seeds and almonds. Heat the oil in a skillet and add the mixture plus the juices left from cooking chicken. Simmer 3 to 5 minutes and add salt to taste. Place chicken back in roasting pan, pour sauce over chicken, then cover and bake in a preheated 350° oven for 20 to 30 minutes—only until tender.

To prepare ahead of time: This can be prepared 1 day before, but do not overcook chicken; cover and refrigerate. Bring to room temperature 2 hours before serving, then reheat, covered, in a preheated 325° oven. This freezes beautifully. Defrost, then reheat, covered, in a preheated 325° oven.

STAN AND DON'S CHICKEN IN PAPAYA

(*serves 4 to 8*)

4 papayas, slightly underripe
1 teaspoon minced dried onion
1 tablespoon cold water
4 tablespoons butter (1/2 stick)
1 cup finely chopped celery
4 tablespoons flour
1 1/2 cups rich chicken stock
1/2 cup heavy whipping cream
3 cups diced cooked chicken
1/2 cup diced pimento
salt and pepper to taste
2 egg yolks
2 tablespoons dry sherry
8 or more saltine crackers, crumbled

Making the chicken filling: Soak dried onion in cold water. Sauté chopped celery in butter 1 minute. Sprinkle with flour, stir, then remove from heat. Add chicken stock and cream, return to heat, and cook, stirring constantly, until mixture begins to boil. Reduce heat, add soaked onion, and simmer for 5 minutes. Add chicken and pimento and heat gently. Add salt and pepper to taste. Beat egg yolks with sherry, add to sauce, and stir over lowest heat for 1 or 2 minutes. Remove from heat and add crumbled saltines—enough to thicken mixture to your taste. Cool to room temperature.

To assemble and serve: Cut papayas in half and remove seeds. Fill cavities with chicken mixture and bake uncovered in a preheated 350° oven for 20 minutes, or until hot. Do not overbake; overcooked papayas become mushy and disintegrate. Serve with forks and spoons and remind guests to eat some papaya with each mouthful of filling.

To prepare ahead of time: Chicken filling can be made 1 day before; cover and refrigerate. Bring to room temperature 2 hours before filling the papayas. Chicken filling can be frozen; be sure to defrost completely and bring to room temperature before baking papayas.

Chicken "Country Captain" Style

(*serves 24*)

5 large onions, finely chopped
1/2 pound butter (2 sticks)
7 green peppers, finely chopped
2 large bunches parsley, chopped (tops only)
2 garlic cloves, mashed (or 2 teaspoons garlic from *garlic oil*, page 28)
salt (2 or 3 teaspoons)
1 teaspoon black pepper
2 teaspoons mace
4 teaspoons curry powder
6 cups canned tomatoes, well mashed
24 large chicken breasts
salt and pepper
flour
oil or vegetable shortening
chicken stock (about 1 cup)
2 cups raisins, soaked in hot water, then drained
3 cups almonds, toasted

Sauté onions in butter, stirring frequently, until lightly browned. Add green pepper and continue cooking 5 more minutes. Add chopped parsley, garlic, salt, pepper, mace, and curry powder, and stir again. Add tomatoes and simmer, stirring occasionally, until mixture thickens—about 30 minutes. Taste for seasoning and set aside.

Season chicken breasts with salt and pepper, then dust with flour. Sauté them in oil or vegetable shortening until well browned. Place chicken in a large roasting pan (or 2) and cover with prepared sauce. If sauce seems too thick, add some chicken stock. Cover tightly and bake in a preheated 325° oven for 30 to 40 minutes—until tender but not overcooked. Arrange chicken on a large hot serving platter. Spoon sauce over chicken, then sprinkle with raisins and almonds.

To prepare ahead of time: This can be prepared 1 day before, but undercook and keep refrigerated; bring to room temperature, then reheat (covered) in a 325° oven. Add almonds and raisins just before serving. This freezes well too; follow directions for day-ahead preparation.

CHICKEN BREASTS IN CORN CHIPS

(*serves 8*)

    8 boned and skinned chicken breasts
    salt and pepper
    1/2 cup melted butter (1 stick)
    2 teaspoons Worcestershire sauce
    1/2-pound bag of corn chips or tortilla chips, ground
      in a food processor or blender

Season chicken with salt and pepper. Combine melted butter and Worcestershire sauce in a bowl and place corn chip (or tortilla chip) crumbs in a pan. Dip chicken in butter sauce, then roll in the chip crumbs and place in a single layer in a large roasting pan. Bake uncovered in a preheated 350° oven for 40 minutes. Baste with the butter sauce and return to oven for about 20 minutes; be careful not to overcook.

To prepare ahead of time: Chicken breasts can be assembled in the morning; keep refrigerated, uncovered, until 2 hours before baking time, then remove from refrigerator to bring to room temperature. Roast as directed.

BONED CHICKEN BREASTS IN PHYLLO

(*serves 8*)

8 boned and skinned chicken breasts
salt and pepper
1/4 pound butter (1 stick)
1/3 cup cognac
1 pound phyllo
1/2 pound melted butter (best if *clarified*, page 28)

for duxelles

    3/4 pound fresh mushrooms
    1 1/2 tablespoons finely chopped shallots (or white bulbs of green onions)
    4 tablespoons butter (1/2 stick)
    salt and pepper to taste
    3 tablespoons madeira or sherry

for sauce

    3 tablespoons fat from top of juices remaining from sautéing chicken
    2 tablespoons flour
    1 1/2 cups chicken broth (including juices from chicken)

Making the duxelles: Finely mince mushrooms (either by hand or in a food processor). Sauté mushrooms and shallots in the butter, stirring over moderate to high heat until all moisture has evaporated and mushrooms have begun to brown. Add salt and pepper, then cook another minute. Add madeira or sherry, and turn off heat, but stir for 1 minute or so. Place in a bowl, cover and refrigerate.

Preparing the chicken: Season chicken with salt and pepper, then quickly sauté in the butter until barely browned, 1/2 to 1 minute for each side—chicken should remain rare. Remove chicken to a large plate or casserole, cover and refrigerate. Add cognac to skillet used for cooking chicken and deglaze the pan, incorporating the brown bits. Pour these juices into a separate bowl to be used later for making the sauce; cover and chill.

To assemble: Unroll phyllo and remove two sheets. (Cover remaining phyllo, first with waxed paper and then with a damp towel, to prevent drying and crumbling.) Brush first sheet with melted butter, top with second sheet and brush it with butter. Place a chicken breast on narrow end of the buttered sheets, then top with a spoonful of duxelles. Roll up, folding in the sides and brushing with butter as you roll. Repeat process for the rest of the chicken. Place wrapped chicken pieces in a greased baking pan (with sides), cover and refrigerate until 1 hour before final baking.

Making the sauce: Melt the fat, stir in flour, then gradually add broth (containing juices from sautéing chicken). Cook over moderate heat, stirring constantly, until sauce comes to a boil. Set aside until time to serve, then reheat gently.

To bake and serve: When ready to bake, place phyllo-wrapped chicken in a preheated 450° oven and bake 10 minutes; reduce heat to 350° and bake about 30 minutes—until pastry is well-browned. Serve on hot dinner plates, spooning sauce at the side of each—not on top, or pastry will become soggy.

To prepare ahead of time: The duxelles can be prepared 2 days before; keep covered and refrigerated. The chicken can be wrapped in phyllo, covered and refrigerated, 1 day before. The sauce too can be made 1 day before. The duxelles can be frozen; defrost completely, but keep it cool until ready to proceed.

Majestic chicken
(*serves 6*)

6 WHOLE chicken breasts, boned but skin left on
salt and pepper
1/4 cup melted butter (1/2 stick)

for the stuffing

    1 onion, finely chopped
    3/4 cup finely chopped celery
    3/4 cup butter (1 1/2 sticks)
    salt and pepper to taste
    4 cups FRESH (not dry!) bread crumbs
    1 1/2 teaspoons poultry seasoning

for mushroom sauce

    1/4 cup fat (left from roasting chicken)
    1/4 pound mushrooms, sliced
    salt and pepper
    2 teaspoons lemon juice
    1 cup rich chicken stock
    1 tablespoon cornstarch
    1/4 cup cold water
    1/3 cup marsala (or sherry)

Making the stuffing: Sauté the chopped onion and celery in the 3/4 cup butter until vegetables are tender and lightly browned. Add bread crumbs and seasonings and mix thoroughly. Set aside.

Roasting the chicken: Open up chicken breasts and season with salt and pepper. Place a large spoonful of stuffing on 1 side of each, then close the breast and fasten with skewers. Place chicken in a large roasting pan in a single layer. Spoon the 1/4 cup melted butter over the chicken and bake in a preheated 350° oven, basting frequently, for about 1 hour or longer. Chicken should be brown and almost tender. Remove skewers.

Making the sauce: Remove 1/4 cup of fat from roasting pan and place in a skillet. Sauté the sliced mushrooms in the fat, adding salt and pepper to taste and the lemon juice. Add chicken stock and simmer 1 or 2 minutes. Dissolve cornstarch in the cold water and add, stirring constantly until mixture boils. Add marsala and set aside.

To assemble: Half an hour before serving, reheat stuffed chicken breasts (covered with foil) in a 350° oven for 10 minutes. Uncover and bake 10 or 15 minutes more, basting once or twice. Spoon prepared hot mushroom sauce over each serving. Excellent served cold too; chill, then slice and serve without the mushroom sauce.

To prepare ahead of time: The stuffing can be prepared 2 days before; cover and keep refrigerated. The chicken breasts can be stuffed and roasted in the morning; leave at room temperature and reserve final baking before serving. The stuffing freezes beautifully; defrost completely, then proceed as directed.

Chicken Breasts with Seedless Grapes

(*serves 12*)

12 chicken breasts
salt and pepper
1/4 pound butter (1 stick)
5 tablespoons flour
1 1/4 cups dry white wine
1 cup chicken stock
1/2 teaspoon onion powder
1/4 teaspoon dried tarragon
1 cup heavy whipping cream
2 cups seedless grapes

Season chicken breasts with salt and pepper. Sauté in butter until browned on both sides, then remove from skillet to a roasting pan. Drain off all but 5 tablespoons of butter from skillet. Add flour and stir, then add white wine and stock and cook over low heat, stirring until sauce comes to a boil. Add onion powder and tarragon. Pour sauce over chicken breasts and cover pan. Bake chicken in a preheated 350° oven for 30 to 45 minutes—just until tender. Remove from oven and place chicken breasts on a warm platter. Add cream to sauce in roasting pan and heat gently without boiling. Pour sauce over chicken and scatter grapes over the top.

To prepare ahead of time: This can be prepared 1 day before; undercook slightly. Cover and refrigerate. Bring to room temperature 2 hours before serving. Heat, covered, in a 300° oven, only until hot. Add grapes just before serving. This can be frozen but without the grapes; follow procedure for day-ahead preparation.

Turkey with Wild Rice Stuffing

(*serves 8 to 10*)

1 turkey (10 to 12 pounds)
salt and pepper
1/2 cup (1 stick) melted butter or oil

for wild rice stuffing

    2 medium-sized onions, finely chopped
    1/4 pound butter (1 stick)
    2 cups chopped celery
    6 cups cooked wild rice (about 2 cups uncooked), or part white rice
    salt and pepper to taste

Making the stuffing: Cook rice. Sauté onion in the butter until lightly browned and tender. Add celery and cook a few minutes longer. Combine with cooked rice and season to taste. Set aside.

Season turkey with salt and pepper and fill cavities with wild rice stuffing. Place turkey in a large roasting pan, pour the melted butter or oil over it and cover the whole turkey loosely with foil. Roast in a preheated 325° oven for 3 1/2 hours or longer—until turkey is well browned and tender. Baste once or twice. More cooking time is needed if turkey and stuffing are cold.

To prepare ahead of time: Stuffing can be prepared 1 day before; cover and refrigerate. The stuffing can be frozen; use promptly after defrosting.

Turkey with Cornbread Stuffing

(*serves 10 to 12*)

1 turkey (14 to 16 pounds)
salt and pepper
1/2 cup (1 stick) melted butter or oil

for cornbread stuffing

4 onions, finely chopped
1/4 pound butter (1 stick)
2 cups finely chopped celery
1 pound pork sausage
4 cups crumbled *cornbread* (page 170)
3 cups bread crumbs
2 or 3 teaspoons poultry seasoning
salt and pepper to taste

Making the stuffing: Sauté the onions in the butter until lightly browned and tender. Add celery and cook a few minutes longer. Remove from skillet and place in large bowl. Brown pork sausage in the skillet and add to onions and celery. Add remaining ingredients and mix thoroughly. Set aside. (This will make more stuffing than is needed to stuff the turkey; put the extra in a separate casserole.)

Season turkey with salt and pepper and fill cavities with stuffing. Place in a large roasting pan, pour butter or oil over the turkey, and cover breast loosely with foil. Place in a 325° oven and roast for 4 1/2 hours or longer, basting occasionally. Turkey should be well browned and tender. If turkey and stuffing are cold, more time will be needed.

To prepare ahead of time: The stuffing can be prepared the day before; cover and refrigerate. The stuffing can be frozen; use promptly after defrosting.

Turkey Mornay on Spinach

(*serves 8*)

8 or more large slices of cooked turkey breast
2 (10-ounce) packages frozen chopped spinach
salt and pepper to taste
butter

for mornay sauce

    2 tablespoons butter
    2 tablespoons flour
    1 cup turkey or chicken stock
    1 cup heavy whipping cream
    salt and pepper to taste
    3/4 cup grated parmesan cheese

Making the sauce: Melt butter, add flour, and stir. Add stock and cook, stirring constantly, until mixture comes to a boil. Add cream, salt, and pepper, and simmer for 5 to 10 minutes. Stir in grated parmesan over lowest heat; if sauce seems too thick, add more cream or stock. Set aside.

Cook spinach 1 or 2 minutes, then drain thoroughly, squeezing out excess liquid. Season with salt, pepper, and butter.

Place cooked spinach in the bottom of a large shallow casserole. Top with turkey slices and cover with the mornay sauce. Place in a preheated 375° oven on the upper shelf and bake until hot and bubbling. For a browner top, place briefly under a broiling unit.

To prepare ahead of time: This can be prepared 1 day before; reserve final baking. Cover and refrigerate, but bring to room temperature 2 hours before serving, then proceed as directed. This can be frozen; defrost completely before baking.

Ducklings with Pineapple

(*serves 4 to 8*)

2 Long Island ducklings
salt and pepper
3 onions, thickly sliced
3 celery stalks, cut in pieces
2 cups duck or chicken stock
2 tablespoons cornstarch
1/4 cup cold water
fresh pineapple slices
melted butter

Remove excess fat from ducklings, then season them inside and out with salt and pepper. Stuff each with some of the onion and celery and place in a roasting pan with remaining onion and celery. Prick skin of the ducklings, cover tightly with pan cover or heavy foil, and roast in a preheated 350° oven for 1 1/2 to 2 hours. Do not uncover during this time.

Remove pan from oven, discard onion and celery, and remove accumulated fat. Increase oven heat to 425°, prick duckling skins again, and return to oven—this time uncovered—for 20 to 30 minutes. Place ducklings on an oven-proof platter and keep warm in a 250° oven.

Making the sauce: Discard fat in roasting pan, add stock and bring to a boil, scraping the brown bits into the stock. Strain into a saucepan. Dissolve cornstarch in the water, add to sauce, and bring to a boil, stirring constantly. Reduce heat and simmer 2 minutes.

Spoon melted butter over pineapple slices and heat in a 425° oven for 5 minutes. Arrange pineapple around ducklings. Carve ducklings or cut with poultry scissors, giving each guest some pineapple slices along with duckling and sauce.

To prepare ahead of time: The ducklings and sauce can be cooked 1 day before; undercook ducklings slightly. Cover and refrigerate. Bring to room temperature 2 hours before serving, then heat ducklings, uncovered, on the upper shelf of a preheated 400° oven. Reheat sauce gently and prepare pineapple as directed.

Ducklings with Peaches

(*serves 6 to 8*)

2 Long Island ducklings, quartered
salt and pepper

for sauce

    1 carrot, chopped
    2 medium-sized onions, chopped
    duck livers, chopped
    1 cup dry red wine
    2 cups duck or chicken stock
    1 tablespoon cornstarch
    1/4 cup cold water
    salt and pepper to taste

8 peach halves (fresh or canned)
finely chopped parsley

Remove excess fat from quartered ducklings, season with salt and pepper, and place them in a roasting pan. Roast, uncovered, in a preheated 400° oven for 30 minutes. Drain off accumulated fat, reduce oven to 325°, cover, and roast 1 to 2 hours longer—until ducklings are almost tender.

Making the sauce: While ducklings are roasting, sauté the chopped carrot, onions, and duck livers in 4 tablespoons of the duck fat removed from the roasting pan. Add the red wine and stock and simmer slowly for 30 minutes. Dissolve cornstarch in the cold water and add to the sauce, stirring until sauce boils. Taste for seasoning. Pour the sauce over the ducklings, cover, and return to a 325° oven for about 30 minutes—until completely tender.

To assemble and serve: Place ducklings on a platter and keep warm in a low oven. Add peaches to the sauce and heat 1 or 2 minutes. Arrange peaches around the ducklings and sprinkle chopped parsley over all. Spoon some of the sauce on the peaches and ducklings and pass remaining sauce in a separate bowl.

To prepare ahead of time: This can be prepared 1 day before, but undercook slightly; cover and refrigerate. Remove from refrigerator 2 hours before serving, then reheat.

Ducklings with Orange Sauce

(*serves 4 to 8*)

2 Long Island ducklings
salt and pepper
2 small onions
2 celery stalks
1 1/2 cups duck or chicken stock
2 tablespoons butter
2 tablespoons flour
juice of 2 oranges
rind of 1 orange
rind of 1 lemon
1/2 cup currant jelly
skinned orange sections

Season ducklings with salt and pepper. Place an onion and some celery in the cavity of each duckling, then place ducklings in a roasting pan. Roast uncovered in a preheated 325° oven for 2 to 3 hours, removing fat as it accumulates. Increase heat to 425° and roast another 30 minutes—until skin is browned and crisp, and ducklings are tender. Remove ducklings to an oven-proof platter; keep warm in a 250° oven.

Making the sauce: Remove fat from roasting pan. Add stock and bring to a boil, scraping the brown bits sticking to the pan into the sauce. In a separate saucepan, melt the butter and stir in the flour, then strain the stock in the roasting pan and add, stirring constantly, until sauce comes to a boil. Add the orange juice and the orange and lemon rinds, and currant jelly. Season to taste and simmer gently for 5 to 10 minutes.

To serve: Place ducklings on a platter, surround with skinned orange segments, and cover with a little of the sauce. Pass the remaining sauce in a separate bowl.

To prepare ahead of time: Ducklings and sauce can be prepared 1 day before. Undercook slightly. Cover and refrigerate separately. Bring to room temperature 2 hours before serving and reheat separately—ducklings in a preheated 300° oven and sauce on top of the stove. Add orange segments just before serving.

Goose with Apple and Prune Stuffing

(*serves 6 to 8*)

1 goose (10 to 12 pounds)
salt and pepper

for stuffing

> 2 onions, finely chopped
> 2 cups finely chopped celery
> 1/4 pound butter (1 stick)
> 2 large apples, peeled and chopped
> 1 1/2 cups diced prunes (soak in water before dicing to soften)
> 2 1/2 to 3 cups dry bread crumbs
> 1/2 cup port
> salt and pepper

Making the stuffing: Sauté onions and celery in the butter. Remove from heat, then add apples, prunes, bread crumbs, and wine. Add salt and pepper to taste and toss well. Cool.

Season goose with salt and pepper, then fill cavity with cooled stuffing. Roast in a preheated 325° oven, covered, for 2 hours. Uncover and remove accumulated fat. Return to oven, uncovered, and roast an additional 2 to 3 hours, until goose is tender. If desired, increase heat to 450° the last 20 minutes to crisp skin.

To prepare ahead of time: The stuffing can be prepared 1 day ahead; keep refrigerated, but bring to room temperature just before stuffing the goose. The stuffing can be frozen; defrost completely before using.

GAME HENS WITH PICADILLO

game hens
picadillo (page 24)
butter
salt and pepper

Season game hens inside with salt and pepper, then fill cavities generously with the picadillo. Place hens in a large shallow roasting pan and rub with melted butter, then season outside of hens with salt and pepper. Place uncovered in a 350° oven and roast for 1 1/2 hours, basting every 20 minutes or so.

To prepare ahead of time: Game hens can be stuffed in the morning; refrigerate until 2 hours before baking, then follow recipe. The picadillo can be frozen as directed in that recipe; be sure it is completely defrosted before stuffing the hens.

GAME HENS WITH RICE-WATERCHESTNUT STUFFING

(*serves 12*)

12 game hens
salt and pepper
1/4 cup vegetable oil
1 cup soy sauce
1/2 cup honey
2 tablespoons grated fresh ginger
3/4 cup stock (from neck and giblets)
1 garlic clove, mashed (or 1 teaspoon garlic from *garlic oil*, page 28)

for rice-waterchestnut stuffing

    1 1/2 cups uncooked rice
    1/4 cup butter (1/2 stick)
    1 onion, finely chopped
    1 green pepper, finely chopped
    salt and pepper to taste
    1 (8-ounce) can waterchestnuts, sliced

Making the stuffing: Cook rice until barely tender—*al dente*. Drain and cool. Sauté onion in the butter until tender but not browned. Add green pepper and sauté another minute. Add salt and pepper to taste, then stir in sliced waterchestnuts. Combine with the rice and mix well.

Season game hens, fill cavities with the rice-waterchestnut stuffing, and place in 2 shallow roasting pans. Rub outside of hens with vegetable oil, then roast uncovered in a preheated 400° oven for 15 minutes. Combine soy sauce, honey, grated ginger, stock, and garlic, and pour over hens. Reduce oven heat to 350° and roast, basting occasionally, for another hour or longer—until hens are tender. Watch that they don't burn; add a little stock or water if necessary.

To prepare ahead of time: The rice-waterchestnut stuffing can be made 2 days before; cover and refrigerate. Bring to room temperature before using. Game hens can be roasted in the morning, but undercook slightly. Cool to room temperature, then cover with foil and leave at room temperature. About 45 minutes before serving, reheat uncovered in a 300° oven, basting occasionally. Add a little stock or water to roasting pans to prevent burning. The rice-waterchestnut stuffing can be frozen; defrost completely before using.

Game Hens with Noodles and Raisins

(serves 12)

12 game hens

for stuffing

       1 (12-ounce) package of 1/4-inch noodles
       1 cup raisins, soaked and drained
       1 cup melted butter (2 sticks)
       2 eggs, slightly beaten
       1/2 teaspoon salt
       1 cup dry white wine
       1 1/2 cups chicken stock
       1 tablespoon cornstarch
       1/4 cup cold water

Making the stuffing: Cook noodles in boiling water until barely tender. Do not overcook. Drain, then place in a bowl and add raisins, 1/2 cup of the melted butter, eggs, and salt. Mix well and set aside.

Season game hens, then fill cavities with the noodle mixture and skewer closed. Place hens in either 1 large roasting pan or 2 small ones. Brush hens with remaining butter, then roast uncovered in a preheated 400° oven for 20 minutes. Reduce heat to 325°, add the wine, and continue roasting for 1 hour or longer—until hens are well browned and tender. Remove hens from roasting pan to a warm platter. Add the chicken stock to roasting pan and deglaze it, scraping the brown bits into the stock. Dissolve cornstarch in the cold water, add to stock, and cook, stirring constantly, until slightly thickened and transparent. Pour sauce over game hens and serve at once.

To prepare ahead of time: The noodle stuffing can be mixed the day before; cover and refrigerate. Bring to room temperature before using. The game hens can be roasted in the morning; cool to room temperature, cover with foil, and leave at room temperature. About 45 minutes before serving, glaze hens with some of the sauce and reheat in a 300° oven. Heat remaining sauce separately.

MEAT

Beef Tenderloins in a Spicy Sauce

(*serves 10*)

- 2 center-cut beef tenderloin roasts (each weighing about 2 1/2 pounds)
- 2 tablespoons oil
- salt and pepper
- 1 onion, thinly sliced
- 1 green pepper, thinly sliced
- 1 lemon, thinly sliced
- 2 teaspoons Worcestershire sauce
- 1 cup ketchup
- 1/2 cup chili sauce
- 1/2 cup dry red wine
- 1 (10 1/2-ounce) can condensed beef bouillon

Roll meat in oil, season with salt and pepper, and place in a large shallow roasting pan. Cover the fat side of each tenderloin with some of the onion, green pepper, and lemon slices. Combine Worcestershire sauce, ketchup, chili sauce, and 2 tablespoons of the red wine and mix well, then spoon over the vegetables. Roast in a preheated 500° oven for 20 minutes, add remaining wine to the pan and baste, then return to oven, reduce heat to 300°, and roast another 20 to 30 minutes. Remove tenderloins to a warm platter. Add beef bouillon to roasting pan and cook over high heat for 1 or 2 minutes. Serve this sauce in a separate bowl; spoon some over each portion as you carve.

To prepare ahead of time: Vegetables and lemon can be sliced 1 day before; refrigerate in a plastic bag. Sauce ingredients can be combined in the morning; leave at room temperature.

Steak in Crêpes with Madeira Sauce
(serves 10)

10 beef tenderloin steaks, 1 1/4 inches thick
medium-ground or cracked black pepper
salt
oil or *clarified butter* (page 28)
10 dinner-plate-size *crêpes* (double recipe, page 27)
5 teaspoons grated parmesan cheese
melted butter
fresh parsley

for mushroom filling

    1 pound fresh mushrooms, sliced
    3 large shallots, finely chopped
    6 tablespoons butter
    4 teaspoons flour
    1/2 cup heavy whipping cream
    1/2 cup madeira
    salt and pepper to taste

for madeira sauce

    1 large onion, chopped
    1 large carrot, chopped
    2 (10 1/2-ounce) cans condensed beef bouillon
    2 teaspoons tomato paste
    2 tablespoons cornstarch
    1/2 cup cold water
    1/4 cup madeira
    salt and pepper to taste

Making the mushroom filling: Sauté shallots in the butter, then add mushrooms and sauté another minute or so. Sprinkle with flour and stir, then add cream and stir constantly until mixture begins to bubble. Reduce heat and season to taste. Add madeira and simmer gently for 1 minute. Remove from heat and cool to room temperature.

Making the madeira sauce: Sauté chopped onion and carrot in butter until tender. Add bouillon and tomato paste, stir, then simmer covered for 15 minutes. Taste for seasoning. Dissolve cornstarch in the water, then add to hot mixture and stir over moderate heat until mixture boils; reduce heat and simmer 30 seconds. Strain, add madeira, and set aside; reheat gently just before serving.

Season steaks by pressing a generous amount of pepper into both sides of steaks with your hands. Sprinkle both sides with salt. Sauté quickly in the oil or clarified butter just until browned: they must remain very rare. Remove from skillet. Place a steak in center of each crêpe and place a small spoonful of mushroom filling on each steak. Wrap crêpes around the meat and place them seam sides down in 2 shallow buttered casseroles. Don't crowd them. Brush tops with melted butter and sprinkle each with 1/2 teaspoon of parmesan. Bake casseroles on the top level of a preheated 450° oven (or ovens) for about 10 minutes; do not overcook. Garnish with parsley and serve at table with the reheated madeira sauce.

To prepare ahead of time: The mushroom filling, the madeira sauce, and the crêpes can be made 1 day ahead; cover and refrigerate separately. Bring mushroom filling to room temperature before wrapping the steaks. The entire dish can be assembled in the early afternoon, covered with plastic wrap, and left at room temperature; proceed with the final heating just before serving. The mushroom filling and madeira sauce can be frozen; defrost completely before using. Crêpes can be frozen as directed in that recipe.

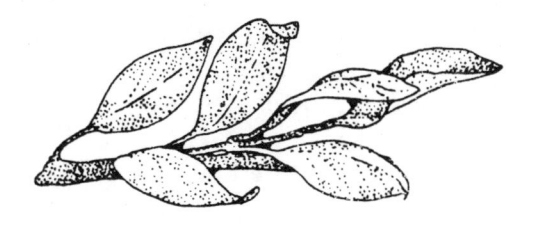

Boiled Beef in the Oven with Horseradish Sauce

(*serves 8 to 12*)

1 (5-pound) beef brisket (middle cut is the leanest)
salt and pepper
4 large carrots, cut in large chunks
2 large onions, cut in pieces
6 celery stalks, cut in chunks
2 (10 1/2-ounce) cans condensed beef bouillon
2 1/2 cups water

for horseradish sauce

> 3 tablespoons butter
> 3 tablespoons flour
> 1 cup of stock (from cooking beef)
> 1/2 cup milk
> salt and pepper, if needed
> 1 tablespoon white wine vinegar
> 2 teaspoons sugar
> 1/4 cup grated horseradish (or to taste)

Season meat generously with salt and pepper and place in a large roasting pan, preferably one with a cover. Surround meat with vegetables, and pour bouillon and water over all. Cover roasting pan with cover (or with heavy foil) and place in a preheated 450° oven for 30 minutes. Reduce heat to 250° and roast another 3 to 4 hours—until tender. Cool, cover, and refrigerate. The next day, remove all fat and slice beef (or leave whole). Reheat and serve as desired—but it is especially good with horseradish sauce.

Making the horseradish sauce: Melt butter, stir in flour, and remove from heat. Add beef stock and milk and stir. Return to heat and stir constantly until mixture boils; reduce heat and simmer gently for 3 minutes. Add vinegar and sugar and bring to a gentle simmer; taste for seasoning. Add horseradish and stir only until hot, then serve.

To prepare ahead of time: This really should be prepared 1 day ahead; it can be made 3 days ahead and kept refrigerated. The sauce can be made 3 days ahead too. This can be frozen; freeze after it has been refrigerated overnight and the excess fat removed.

Beef short ribs with sauerkraut

(*serves 4*)

    3 pounds lean beef short ribs
    salt and pepper
    1 pound sauerkraut, rinsed and drained
    1 onion, sliced

Season ribs with salt and pepper and place on top of sauerkraut and onions in a roasting pan. Place under a broiling unit and broil ribs until lightly browned, about 5 minutes. Cover pan tightly with foil, then roast at 275° for 2 to 3 hours—until tender.

To prepare ahead of time: This can be prepared 2 days ahead; keep covered and refrigerated. To serve, bring to room temperature, cover with foil, and heat in a 300° oven.

Indonesian Lamb Roasts with Peaches and Chutney

(*serves 8*)

4 (6-rib) lamb racks, cut so that 3 chops are joined together

for marinade

    1/4 cup vinegar
    rind and juice of 1 lemon
    1 garlic clove, mashed (or 1 teaspoon garlic from *garlic oil*, page 28)
    1 tablespoon dehydrated minced onion
    1 teaspoon celery seeds
    1 teaspoon oregano
    2 bay leaves
    2 tablespoons soy sauce
    1 teaspoon salt
    2 teaspoons A-1 sauce
    2 tablespoons curry powder
    2 dashes Tabasco sauce
    1/3 cup dijon-style mustard
    1/3 cup honey
    1/4 cup oil

8 canned peach halves
1 cup mango chutney

Combine all ingredients for the marinade in a bowl and mix thoroughly, then set aside. Place lamb chops in a large roasting pan in a single layer and spoon marinade over chops. Leave at room temperature for 2 hours or longer. Drain marinade from chops and reserve. Roast chops, fat sides up, in a preheated 450° oven for 15 minutes, baste with some of the reserved marinade, and return to oven for 10 minutes longer. Heat remaining reserved marinade and serve as a sauce with the lamb roasts. Accompany with peach halves filled with chutney.

To prepare ahead of time: The marinade can be made 1 month ahead; keep tightly covered and refrigerated.

Leg of Lamb with Potatoes and Onions

(*serves about 6*)

1 leg of lamb
garlic oil (page 28)
2 onions, sliced
4 large potatoes, peeled and sliced 1/2 inch thick
2 cups rich stock (undiluted canned bouillon is fine)
salt and pepper

Rub lamb with garlic oil, season with salt and pepper, and place in a large roasting pan. Surround lamb with sliced onions and potatoes and roast in a preheated 350° oven for 45 minutes. Add stock to pan and roast another 45 minutes, basting once or twice. Serve each guest some of the potatoes, onions, and juices with the lamb.

To prepare ahead of time: Potatoes and onions can be peeled in the morning; place them in a bowl of cold water. Lamb and vegetables can also be cooked, if desired, in the morning, but undercook by about 15 or 20 minutes; leave at room temperature, lightly covered with foil. Return to oven in the evening, baste and finish roasting.

Perfectly Easy Racks of Lamb

(*serves 4 to 6*)

2 (6- to 8-rib) lamb racks, well trimmed of fat; bone ends trimmed of fat and gristle
salt and pepper

Season lamb with salt and pepper. Place lamb racks in a roasting pan, fat sides up. Roast in a preheated 450° oven for 15 minutes; baste with fat in pan, reduce heat to 425°, and return to oven for 10 minutes longer. Remove to a serving platter or cutting board and carve at table.

To prepare ahead of time: Remember to ask your butcher to prepare the lamb racks for easy carving: ask him to remove the chine bone, trim away the fat, and scrape the ends of the bones.

Baked Lamb Chops

(*serves 4*)

4 thick loin lamb chops
1 envelope dried onion soup
1/2 cup thinly sliced celery
1 large tomato (8 slices)
4 pieces heavy-duty foil (8 by 12 inches)

Place 1 lamb chop on each piece of foil. Top each with a heaping tablespoon of dried onion soup, then with some celery and 2 tomato slices. Fold edges of foil together and seal. Place in a baking pan and bake in a preheated 450° oven for 10 minutes; reduce heat to 350° and bake about 30 minutes more. Serve each guest his own packet to open.

To prepare ahead of time: The packets can be assembled 1 day ahead; keep refrigerated. Bring to room temperature about 3 hours before baking, then proceed as directed.

My Favorite Lamb Stew

(*serves 6 to 8*)

4 pounds lean lamb stew meat, cut in 2-inch pieces
4 tablespoons butter (1/2 stick)
2 large onions, chopped
5 tablespoons flour
2 cups canned tomatoes
1/2 teaspoon basil
1/4 teaspoon oregano
1/4 teaspoon rosemary
salt and pepper to taste
1 cup sour cream
chopped fresh parsley

Melt butter in a large skillet or Dutch oven and sauté lamb for 2 minutes, turning frequently. Add onions and sauté another minute, then add flour and stir well. Add tomatoes and herbs, and season with salt and pepper. Cover, turn heat to lowest simmer, and cook for about 2 hours or until lamb is tender but not overcooked. (If desired, use a 300° oven instead.) Remove from heat, stir in sour cream and heat only until hot; do not boil. Serve garnished with chopped parsley.

To prepare ahead of time: This can be made 2 days before; keep refrigerated. Reheat gently, stirring occasionally, then serve. This stew freezes beautifully; defrost completely, then reheat over low heat, stirring occasionally.

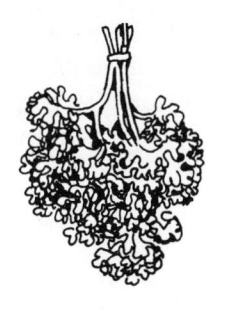

Rack of Veal Madeira

(*serves 6 to 8*)

1 rack of veal, trimmed (containing about 6 ribs)
salt and pepper
1 onion, chopped
2 carrots, chopped
2 celery stalks, chopped
1/2 cup melted butter (1 stick)
2 cups of rich stock
1/2 cup madeira

Season veal with salt and pepper, then place in a roasting pan on top of the chopped onions, carrots, and celery. Pour melted butter over veal and place uncovered in a preheated 450° oven for 20 minutes. Reduce heat to 350° and baste twice during an additional hour of roasting. Add stock to pan and continue to roast, basting occasionally, for about 30 minutes (depending on temperature of veal when you began). Veal should be somewhat pink; do not overcook. Remove veal from oven and place on a warm platter. Add madeira to roasting pan and deglaze over moderate heat, scraping in the good brown bits that cling to the pan. Serve this pan sauce with slices of the veal.

Note: The sauce can, if desired, be strained and thickened. Dissolve a little cornstarch in some cold water, then add it gradually to the boiling sauce, stirring constantly, until you have the consistency you want.

To prepare ahead of time: The vegetables can be chopped 1 day ahead; keep refrigerated in a plastic bag. The veal can be roasted and sauce prepared in the morning; undercook veal slightly. Leave both at room temperature. Reheat veal in the oven before serving and reheat sauce separately.

Veal Chops Italian Style

(*serves 6*)

    6 loin or rib veal chops, cut 1 1/4 inches thick
    salt and pepper
    olive oil
    1/4 pound butter, softened (1 stick)
    lemon wedges

Season chops with salt and pepper and rub with olive oil. Broil or barbecue for about 7 minutes on one side and 5 minutes on the other; do not overcook. Veal should still be pink inside. Place on a very hot platter and cover each with some of the soft butter. Serve with lemon wedges.

To prepare ahead of time: Most important is to find a meat market that has fine-quality veal.

Veal chops marsala

(*serves 6*)

    6 loin or rib veal chops, cut 1 1/4 inches thick
    1/2 cup flour
    2 teaspoons salt
    1/4 teaspoon pepper
    1/8 teaspoon paprika
    6 tablespoons butter
    1/3 pound fresh mushrooms, sliced
    3/4 cup condensed beef bouillon
    3/4 cup dry marsala
    1/4 cup grated parmesan cheese

Combine flour, salt, pepper, and paprika and mix well. Dip veal chops into this mixture, covering them well, then shake off (but do not discard) excess. Sauté the chops in 4 tablespoons of the butter over moderate heat, turning them occasionally until they are lightly browned. Place chops in an oven-proof casserole or roasting pan and set aside. Add remaining butter to skillet and sauté the mushrooms for 1 or 2 minutes. Sprinkle 2 tablespoons of the seasoned flour mixture over mushrooms and stir, then add bouillon and marsala and stir constantly until mixture comes to a boil. Pour mushrooms and sauce over chops, cover tightly with foil, and bake in a preheated 300° oven for 40 minutes, turning once during the baking. Set aside at room temperature until 1 hour before serving time.

To finish: Bake chops uncovered in a 300° oven for 1 hour, basting every 20 minutes. Spoon parmesan on top of each chop and spoon some of the sauce over the parmesan, then return to oven and bake 8 minutes longer.

To prepare ahead of time: This can be prepared in the morning, or 1 day before, up to the point of the final baking. Keep refrigerated, but remove from refrigerator 2 hours before the final baking.

Mexican Pork in Green Sauce

(serves about 10)

6 pounds lean, boneless pork, cut in 2-inch cubes
3 tablespoons oil
2 onions, chopped
2 cups dry-roasted sunflower seeds
2/3 cup dry-roasted, unsalted peanuts
2 (10-ounce) cans tomatillos, drained
2 (7-ounce) cans green chile salsa

Sauté pork cubes in oil over high heat until browned, then add onion and sauté another 2 minutes. Place in a large casserole. Grind sunflower seeds and peanuts in a food processor until finely ground and add to the pork. Purée tomatillos in food processor and add to pork along with the chile salsa. Cover and roast in a preheated 250° oven for several hours, until pork is tender. Taste for salt; it probably won't need any since the sunflower seeds are salty.

To prepare ahead of time: This can be made 2 days ahead; refrigerate. Reheat in a 300° oven only until very hot. This freezes well, too; defrost, then reheat in a 300° oven until hot but not overcooked.

Stuffed Pork Chops with Mustard Sauce

(*serves 6*)

6 loin pork chops, cut 1 1/2 inches thick
salt and pepper to taste
2 tablespoons butter
1 cup rich stock

for stuffing

4 tablespoons butter (1/2 stick)
1 onion, finely chopped
1 cup finely chopped celery
1 cup dry bread crumbs
1 egg, slightly beaten
salt and pepper to taste

for mustard sauce

reserved juices from the baked pork chops
1 1/2 tablespoons cornstarch
1/4 cup cold water
2 to 3 teaspoons prepared mustard
2 tablespoons vinegar
1/4 cup heavy whipping cream

Making the stuffing: Sauté onion and celery in the butter until lightly browned, then add bread crumbs and stir well. Add egg, stir, and season to taste. Remove from heat and cool.

Preparing the pork chops: Cut a large slit in each chop on the wide side. Stuff each with a few spoonfuls of the stuffing and skewer the chops closed. Sauté stuffed chops in the 2 tablespoons of butter until lightly browned on each side, then transfer them to a roasting pan. Add rich stock to the skillet in which chops were sautéed, and stir. Pour over the chops, cover tightly, and bake in a preheated 325° oven for about 1 hour, or until tender. Remove from oven, remove skewers, and place chops on a warm oven-proof platter. Reserve juices for the sauce.

Making the mustard sauce: Combine cornstarch with the cold water and stir well. Place all ingredients except cream in a saucepan and cook over low heat, stirring constantly, until sauce comes to a boil. Add cream, stir, and remove from heat.

To serve: If necessary, cover chops and reheat briefly in the oven. Serve with some mustard sauce spooned over each chop.

To prepare ahead of time: This can be prepared 1 day before. Pour sauce over baked chops and refrigerate. Bring to room temperature several hours before serving; cover with foil and reheat in a 350° oven only until hot. This can also be frozen after chops have been baked; cover with sauce and wrap well before freezing. To serve, defrost completely, then cover with foil and reheat in a 350° oven only until very hot.

Spareribs Teriyaki

(*serves about 6*)

5 pounds pork spareribs
salt and pepper
1 1/2 cups dry white wine

for teriyaki sauce

    1 cup soy sauce
    1 cup dry white wine
    1/2 cup sugar
    1 garlic clove, mashed (or 1 teaspoon garlic from
       garlic oil, page 28)
    1 (2-inch) piece fresh ginger, peeled and chopped

Making the teriyaki sauce: Combine all ingredients and stir until sugar has dissolved.

Season spareribs with salt and pepper, then place them in a very large roasting pan. Bake uncovered in a preheated 450° oven for 30 minutes. Remove any accumulated fat from pan, then pour teriyaki sauce and the 1 1/2 cups wine over the ribs. Cover pan with heavy-duty foil and return to oven, reducing heat to 275°. Roast, basting and turning ribs occasionally, until tender—about 1 1/2 to 2 hours longer.

To prepare ahead of time: The teriyaki sauce can be made up to 1 month ahead, but it must be kept in a tightly sealed jar in the refrigerator. The spareribs can be cooked 2 days ahead and kept refrigerated. They freeze well too.

Special entrées

Spaghetti Carbonara, My Version

(*serves 2 to 4*)

1/2 pound spaghetti
1/2 pound bacon
3 eggs
1 tablespoon milk or cream
3/4 teaspoon salt
1/4 teaspoon pepper
3 to 4 green onions, finely chopped
grated parmesan cheese

Dice bacon and sauté until crisp; set skillet aside but do *not* drain: you will need the fat. Beat eggs and milk together in a bowl. Cook spaghetti to the *al dente* stage, then drain; return spaghetti to the pot. Add hot bacon and fat (reheating if necessary) and toss quickly. Remove from heat, add salt and pepper, beaten egg–milk mixture, and green onions; toss again and bring to table in the pot, or place on a hot platter. Serve on heated plates and pass grated parmesan separately.

To prepare ahead of time: Ingredients can be assembled in the morning, and the bacon can be cooked. If you have everything ready at the stove, you have only to cook the spaghetti, add ingredients, and serve.

Springtime Spaghetti

(*serves 2 to 4*)

1 cup raw carrot chunks
1 1/2 cups celery slices
1 cup fresh parsley (measure after removing stems)
2 cups watercress (measure after removing stems)
1 1/2 cups chopped fresh tomatoes
3/4 cup olive oil
2 teaspoons mashed garlic (or from *garlic oil*, page 28)
1 3/4 teaspoons salt
1 teaspoon freshly ground pepper
1/2 pound thin spaghetti

Chop carrots, celery, parsley, watercress, and tomatoes finely, either by hand, or by putting each vegetable—separately—into a food processor (be careful not to purée the vegetables). Place chopped vegetables in a bowl and add oil, garlic, salt, and pepper. Cook spaghetti in salted water until *al dente*, drain, then return to pot, add vegetable-oil mixture, and toss over low heat for 1 or 2 minutes, only long enough to heat but not cook vegetables. Serve on warm plates.

To prepare ahead of time: Vegetables can be chopped 1 day before and oil added; cover and refrigerate. Bring to room temperature 3 hours before serving.

Fettucine Alfredo-Mellinkoff

(*serves 4 as a main course, 6 or 8 as a first course*)

for sauce

      1/2 pound butter (2 sticks)
      2 cups heavy whipping cream
      1 teaspoon salt
      1/2 teaspoon pepper
      1/2 pound grated imported parmesan cheese

for pasta

      12 ounces fettucine
      8 quarts water
      2 tablespoons oil
      2 tablespoons salt

Making the sauce: Melt the butter in a saucepan, but do not let it cook. Add the cream over lowest heat, barely warm it, then remove from heat. Stir in salt, pepper, and grated parmesan. Set aside.

Cooking the pasta: Bring the water to a boil in a very large pot, then add oil and salt. Add fettucine and cook until barely tender (*al dente*). Drain but do not rinse. Return fettucine to the large pot, add the sauce, then toss over lowest heat for 1 or 2 minutes. Serve on heated plates.

To prepare ahead of time: The sauce can be prepared in the morning. Cover and leave at room temperature.

Lasagne Rolls

(*makes 16 to 18 rolls*)

1 pound commercial lasagne pasta (about 18 strips, 10 inches long)

for sauce

    1 large onion, chopped
    1 garlic clove, mashed (or 1 teaspoon garlic from *garlic oil*, page 28)
    2 tablespoons oil
    1 (1-pound) can tomatoes
    3 (8-ounce) cans tomato sauce
    1/2 teaspoon basil
    1/4 teaspoon thyme
    salt and pepper to taste

for filling

    1 (10-ounce) package frozen chopped spinach, defrosted and drained
    1 1/2 pounds ricotta cheese
    1 cup grated parmesan cheese
    2 eggs
    1 1/4 to 1 1/2 teaspoons salt
    1/4 teaspoon pepper
    1/4 teaspoon nutmeg

Making the sauce: Sauté onion and garlic in the oil until lightly browned. Add remaining ingredients, cover and simmer for 30 minutes.

Making the filling: Place spinach in food processor and whirl only long enough to chop it a little more. Add remaining ingredients and process until combined.

To assemble: Cook lasagne until barely tender, then drain and rinse with cold water. Lay strips on towels to dry them thoroughly. Place about 3 tablespoons of filling on each strip and spread evenly, then roll up (jelly-roll fashion) and place in single layers in shallow casseroles. Cover with foil.

To bake: Place covered rolls in a preheated 350° oven for 10 minutes, then remove, uncover, and spoon 2 tablespoons of sauce over each roll. Cover lightly, return to oven and bake another 10 to 15 minutes. Serve hot, spooning additional sauce over each portion. Grated parmesan can be passed at table.

To prepare ahead of time: Rolls can be assembled and sauce made 1 day before; refrigerate separately. Remove from refrigerator 2 hours before serving, then proceed as in recipe. This freezes too; freeze filled rolls and sauce separately. Defrost completely and bring to room temperature, before proceeding.

CRABMEAT ENCHILADAS

(*makes 10 to 12*)

10 to 12 corn tortillas
vegetable oil
3/4 pound crabmeat
9 to 10 ounces jack cheese, grated
8 green onions, chopped
1 (8-ounce) carton sour cream
1/2 cup mayonnaise
salt and pepper to taste

for sauce

> 1/4 cup butter (1/2 stick)
> 1/4 cup flour
> 2 (10-ounce) cans enchilada sauce
> 1 (10 1/2-ounce) can condensed beef bouillon
> 1/4 cup water
> 1/2 teaspoon oregano
> 1/2 teaspoon ground cumin
> 2 teaspoons chicken stock concentrated base

for garnish

> additional sour cream
> chopped green onions

Making the sauce: Melt butter, then stir in flour and cook over low heat for 1 minute. Remove from heat and when bubbling stops, add remaining ingredients. Return to heat and bring to a boil, stirring constantly. Reduce heat and simmer for 5 minutes. Set aside at room temperature.

Making the enchiladas: Combine crabmeat, cheese, green onions, sour cream, and mayonnaise in a bowl; season to taste. Heat oil in a small skillet to a depth of 1/4 inch. Dip each tortilla in the oil (at moderate temperature) only long enough to soften, then stack them between paper towels. Place a large spoonful of crabmeat mixture on each tortilla, roll up, and place seam-side down in a single layer in 1 or 2 shallow casseroles. Cover with prepared sauce and bake, uncovered, in a preheated 350° oven for 20 minutes, or until hot and bubbling. Garnish tops of enchiladas with additional sour cream and chopped onion.

To prepare ahead of time: Tortillas can be filled 1 day before, covered and refrigerated. Sauce can be made 2 days before and kept refrigerated. Bring both to room temperature, then proceed as the recipe directs. Filled tortillas and sauce can be frozen separately; defrost each completely, then proceed as directed. Frozen enchiladas will be delicious, but their texture will be less chewy.

Twenty-Four Chicken Enchiladas

24 corn tortillas
2 large frying chickens
2 onions
salt and pepper
2 pounds jack cheese, grated
2 (4 1/2-ounce) cans chopped ripe olives, drained
2 bunches green onions, chopped
vegetable oil

for sauce

1/4 pound butter (1 stick)
1/2 cup flour
2 (10-ounce) cans enchilada sauce
6 to 7 cups chicken broth (left from cooking chicken)

for garnish

sour cream
ripe olives

Cooking the chicken: Place chickens in a large pot with salt, pepper, onions, and water to cover. Simmer gently for 1 hour or until tender. Remove from heat and cool to room temperature. Drain, reserving broth for sauce. Remove skin and bones from chicken, then dice chicken and set aside.

Making the sauce: Melt butter and stir in flour. Gradually add enchilada sauce and chicken broth and stir until mixture comes to a boil. Simmer for 5 minutes, then taste for seasoning.

Assembling the enchiladas: Combine in a bowl the diced chicken, ripe olives, jack cheese, and green onions; add salt and pepper to taste. Heat oil in a skillet and dip tortillas in hot oil only long enough to soften, then remove and stack them between paper towels. Place a heaping spoonful of chicken mixture on each and roll up. Place seam-side down in shallow casseroles, cover with sauce, and bake uncovered in a 350° oven for 20 to 30 minutes. Garnish with sour cream and ripe olives.

To prepare ahead of time: These can be prepared 1 day before, but refrigerate filled tortillas and sauce separately; bring to room temperature, then proceed as in recipe. Filled tortillas and sauce can be frozen separately; defrost, add sauce, and heat as directed.

BEEF BURRITOS

(makes 8 to 12)

8 to 10 large flour tortillas
1 large garlic clove, mashed (or 1 teaspoon garlic from *garlic oil*, page 28)
1 large onion, chopped
4 tablespoons oil
3 cups diced cooked beef (leftover roast or boiled)
1 1/2 teaspoons ground cumin
1 (7-ounce) can green chile salsa
4 cups refried beans (canned are fine)
salt and pepper to taste

Sauté garlic and onion in the oil until lightly browned. Add cubed beef and sauté for 1 or 2 minutes. Add cumin and chile salsa and stir well, then add refried beans, season to taste, cover, and simmer for 45 minutes. (Or you can bake this in a covered casserole in a preheated 350° oven for 1 hour.) Remove from heat and cool; if time permits, refrigerate before filling tortillas. Place a large spoonful on each flour tortilla, roll up, turning in sides, and place each on a large piece of foil; wrap securely.

To serve: Place foil-wrapped burritos in a preheated 350° oven for 30 minutes. If you like the outside dry and crisp, remove foil wrapping after 15 minutes.

To prepare ahead of time: These can be prepared 3 days ahead; keep refrigerated. If they are cold, the oven baking will take longer. These burritos freeze magnificently; defrost and bake as directed (allow more time if cold or partially frozen).

Green Corn Tamales Simplified

(makes about 12)

dry corn husks (need at least 24)
3 (10-ounce) packages frozen whole-kernel corn
2 teaspoons salt
1/4 cup melted butter (1/2 stick)
1 to 1 1/4 cups yellow cornmeal
12 strips of cheddar cheese (about 1/2 by 2 inches)
12 strips of jack cheese (about 1/2 by 2 inches)
1 (7-ounce) can whole green chiles, seeds removed and cut in strips

for sauce

1 (7-ounce) can green chile salsa
1 (1-pound) can tomatoes

Clean corn husks and soak them for several hours (or overnight) in water, then drain thoroughly. Defrost whole-kernel corn, then whirl in a food processor until almost, but not quite, puréed. Remove to a bowl and add salt, butter, and cornmeal, and stir until well combined. Arrange 2 corn husks so they overlap (1 with the point upward and the other with the point downward; if necessary, use a tiny bit of the corn mixture to hold them in place). Spread the center with about 2 tablespoons of the corn mixture and top each with a strip of the 2 cheeses and 1 strip of chile. Fold in sides of husks and then fold up so their points meet. If tamales do not hold together, tie with string. Place on a rack in a large steamer or pot or large roasting pan. Pour 1 inch of boiling water in bottom of pan, cover, and steam 1 hour or until tamales are firm. Serve hot with the sauce.

Making the sauce: Combine ingredients in a saucepan and simmer together for 3 minutes. Serve hot over the tamales.

To prepare ahead of time: Both the tamales and the sauce can be made 2 days ahead; keep refrigerated. Reheat tamales by wrapping them in double foil and placing in a 350° oven until hot, or steam them again as directed in recipe until piping hot. Reheat sauce, stirring gently.

Gougère

(*serves 8 to 10*)

1/2 cup milk
1/2 cup water
1/4 pound butter (1 stick)
1 teaspoon salt
1/8 teaspoon pepper
1/8 teaspoon nutmeg
1 cup sifted flour (4 1/2 ounces)
4 eggs
1 1/4 cups diced jack or cheddar cheese

Bring milk, water, butter, salt, pepper, and nutmeg to a boil, then add flour all at once and stir vigorously over low heat until mixture forms a ball and leaves the sides of the pan. Stir over lowest heat for about a minute, then remove from heat and cool for several minutes. Beat in eggs 1 at a time, fully incorporating each egg before adding another. Stir in 1 cup of the diced cheese and cool slightly.

Grease a large cookie tin with vegetable shortening. Place egg-sized scoops of dough on the tin in the shape of a ring about 12 inches in diameter, leaving a space in the middle 5 inches in diameter. Then, using a teaspoon, scoop smaller ovals and place on top of the large ones. Sprinkle remaining 1/4 cup cheese on top of the gougère, and bake in a preheated 400° oven for 15 minutes. Reduce heat to 350° and bake an additional 30 to 40 minutes. Serve hot.

To prepare ahead of time: The dough can be prepared in the morning; refrigerate until an hour before baking, then form into a ring as directed. Or the gougère can be completely assembled on the baking tin and refrigerated. Remove from refrigerator 1 hour before time to bake.

Spinach Roll with Scrambled Eggs and Mushroom Sauce

(*serves about 6*)

for spinach roll

    2 tablespoons butter
    1 tablespoon flour
    1/3 cup milk
    2 teaspoons minced dried onion
    salt and pepper to taste
    2 teaspoons lemon juice
    2 (10-ounce) packages frozen chopped spinach, defrosted and thoroughly drained
    4 egg yolks
    4 egg whites
    1/4 cup grated parmesan cheese
    1/2 cup dry bread crumbs

for scrambled eggs

    6 eggs
    3 tablespoons milk
    1/4 cup butter (1/2 stick)
    salt and pepper to taste

for mushroom sauce

    1/2 pound fresh mushrooms, sliced
    1/4 cup butter (1/2 stick)
    salt and pepper
    2 teaspoons lemon juice
    1 tablespoon flour
    2/3 cup heavy whipping cream

Making the mushroom sauce: Sauté mushrooms in the butter, then season with salt, pepper, and lemon juice. Sprinkle with flour, stir, then add cream and cook, stirring constantly, until mixture boils. Reduce heat and simmer for 1 minute. Set aside; reheat later.

Making the spinach roll: Melt butter, stir in flour, then add milk and onion and cook, stirring constantly, until mixture bubbles. Reduce heat and add salt, pepper, lemon juice, and drained spinach. Simmer for 1 minute. Beat egg yolks, then add to spinach and set aside. Beat egg whites until stiff but not dry and fold into spinach mixture. Butter a baking pan (10 by 15 inches) and line with waxed paper; butter paper too and sprinkle with the bread crumbs. Pour in the spinach mixture, sprinkle with the grated parmesan, and bake in a preheated 350° oven for 15 to 20 minutes. Remove from oven and turn out upside down on greased waxed paper or foil. Remove paper from the baked spinach.

Making the scrambled eggs: Assemble all ingredients at the stove while spinach is baking. Combine eggs, milk, salt, and pepper. Melt butter in a skillet, add eggs and scramble only until they are creamy; do not overcook.

To assemble and serve: Cover spinach with scrambled eggs and roll up with the aid of the paper or foil. Place on a warm platter, and serve the reheated mushroom sauce at the side.

To prepare ahead of time: The spinach mixture can be baked in the morning; leave at room temperature. To serve, reheat (covered with foil) in a low oven, then proceed as directed in recipe. The mushroom sauce can be prepared 2 days ahead; keep covered and refrigerated. Reheat briefly before serving with spinach roll.

Smoked Turkey Omelet

(*serves 2 to 4*)

6 eggs
3 tablespoons water
1/2 teaspoon salt
1/8 teaspoon pepper
4 tablespoons butter (1/2 stick)
3 tablespoons grated parmesan cheese

for filling

1 onion, chopped
1/2 green pepper, chopped
salt and pepper to taste
1 1/2 cups cubed smoked turkey
2 tablespoons butter

Preparing the filling: Sauté onion in the 2 tablespoons butter until limp and lightly browned. Add green pepper and sauté another minute or so. Season with salt and pepper, then add cubed turkey and cook just long enough to heat turkey. Set aside to reheat later.

Preparing the omelet: Beat eggs slightly with the water, salt, and pepper. Melt the 4 tablespoons butter in a very large nonstick skillet and add the eggs. Cook as for any omelet. While cooking the eggs, reheat the vegetable-turkey mixture. Place mixture in center of omelet, sprinkle with the parmesan and fold. Turn out on a warm serving platter and serve as quickly as possible.

To prepare ahead of time: The vegetable-turkey mixture can be prepared the day before; keep covered and refrigerated. Bring to room temperature before cooking the omelet, and reheat as directed in the recipe.

WILD RICE, PINE NUTS, AND CURRANTS

(serves 12)

    1 pound wild rice
    1/4 pound butter (1 stick)
    2 large onions, chopped
    1/2 cup currants, covered with boiling water, then
       drained and dried on paper towels
    1 1/2 cups pine nuts, lightly toasted in oven
    salt and pepper to taste

Cook wild rice, drain, and set aside. Sauté chopped onion in the butter until tender and lightly browned. Add currants and pine nuts and sauté over moderate heat for 2 minutes. Remove from heat and combine with cooked rice. Add salt and pepper to taste and mix well. About 30 minutes before serving, cover with foil and heat in a 350° oven.

To prepare ahead of time: This can be prepared 2 days ahead, covered and refrigerated. Bring to room temperature several hours before final oven heating. This freezes well; defrost completely, then heat as directed.

Fruited Rice

(*serves about 12*)

6 cups cooked rice (about 2 cups uncooked)
1 cup raisins
2 cups dried apricots
1 large onion, chopped
1 green pepper, chopped
1/4 pound butter (1 stick)
salt and pepper to taste

Soak raisins in hot water for 10 minutes, drain, then dry on paper towels. Soak apricots in hot water for 20 minutes, drain, dry on paper towels, then cut in 1/2-inch pieces. Sauté chopped onion and green pepper in butter for a few minutes, then add rice, raisins, and apricots and season with salt and pepper. Place in a casserole and cover lightly with foil. Heat in a preheated 375° oven for about 30 minutes—or until very hot.

To prepare ahead of time: This can be prepared 2 days ahead, covered and refrigerated, or it can be frozen. Bring to room temperature before the final oven heating.

Vegetables

Asparagus, a Chinese Way

(serves 12)

    6 pounds fresh asparagus
    4 tablespoons vegetable oil
    1 garlic clove, mashed (or 1 teaspoon garlic from *garlic oil*, page 28)
    1 1/2-inch piece fresh ginger, peeled and finely chopped
    salt and pepper to taste

Break or cut off tough ends of the asparagus, then peel the stems with a potato peeler and slice asparagus diagonally into 3/4-inch pieces. Heat oil in a large heavy pot. Add garlic and ginger, then add asparagus slices and toss and fry over highest heat for 1 or 2 minutes. Season, then remove from heat and serve.

To prepare ahead of time: The asparagus can be cleaned and sliced 1 day ahead; keep refrigerated in a tightly sealed plastic bag.

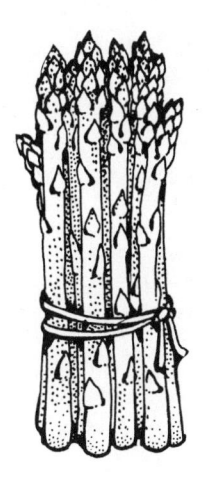

Four Vegetables with Cheese Sauce

(*serves about 12*)

4 cups sliced raw zucchini
4 cups shelled fresh peas
1 medium-size cauliflower, divided into flowerets
1 pound fresh green beans, cut in 1-inch pieces

for cheese sauce

2 tablespoons butter
2 tablespoons flour
1 1/2 cups milk
2 cups grated cheddar cheese
1/2 teaspoon salt
dash of cayenne pepper

Making the cheese sauce: Melt butter and stir in flour. Gradually stir in milk and cook over low heat, stirring constantly, until sauce comes to a boil. Reduce heat and simmer 1 minute. Add cheese, salt, and cayenne and stir over low heat until cheese has melted. If sauce is too thick, add a little more milk.

Cook cauliflower in boiling water for 2 minutes, then drain. Do the same with the green beans. Both vegetables should remain very crisp. Using either 1 very large shallow casserole or 2 small ones, arrange the 4 vegetables in separate sections—do not mix them together. Cover with cheese sauce and bake in a preheated 350° oven for 15 or 20 minutes.

To prepare ahead of time: This can be assembled 1 day ahead; finish baking shortly before serving.

Braised Red Cabbage

(*serves 6 to 8*)

    1 solid head red cabbage (2 to 2 1/2 pounds)
    1/4 cup lemon juice
    1/2 cup dry red wine
    1/4 cup butter (1/2 stick)
    2 tablespoons sugar
    1 1/2 teaspoons salt
    1/2 cup red currant jelly
    1 tart apple, peeled and finely chopped

Wash cabbage and remove tough outer leaves, then shred or slice finely. Combine lemon juice, wine, butter, sugar, and salt in a heat-proof casserole; bring to a boil over direct heat and add cabbage, apple, and jelly. Toss and bring to a boil again, then cover tightly and braise in a preheated 325° oven for 2 1/2 hours. Stir once or twice during the cooking. If cabbage becomes dry, add 1 or 2 tablespoons of boiling water.

To prepare ahead of time: This can be prepared 3 days ahead; keep covered and refrigerated. Reheat to serve. It freezes well; defrost and reheat to serve.

Carrots and Celery

(*serves about 4*)

2 tablespoons butter
1 small onion, finely chopped
1 cup finely chopped carrots
2 cups finely chopped celery
salt and pepper to taste

Heat butter in a large skillet and sauté onion for 2 minutes. Add carrots and sauté another 1 or 2 minutes, stirring occasionally. Add celery and sauté 1 minute, then add salt and pepper to taste. Cover skillet, reduce heat, and cook for 3 minutes.

To prepare ahead of time: This can be prepared 1 day ahead; cover and refrigerate. Bring to room temperature about 2 hours before serving. Reheat over moderate heat, stirring constantly, only until hot.

Medley of White Corn and Celery

(*serves about 8*)

3 cups finely chopped celery
1/4 pound butter (1 stick)
2 (12-ounce) cans white shoe peg corn (3 1/2 cups drained)
salt and pepper to taste
4 green onions, chopped

Sauté celery in the butter briefly—until barely tender but still crisp. Add corn and simmer 1 minute. Season with salt and pepper, then stir in the chopped green onion.

To prepare ahead of time: This can be prepared 1 day ahead; cover and refrigerate. Bring to room temperature 2 hours before serving, then reheat in a large skillet or pot, stirring over high heat only long enough to heat.

Simply Baked Corn

(serves 4 to 6)

2 (10-ounce) packages frozen whole kernel corn, defrosted
3/4 teaspoon salt
2 eggs

Grind corn in a food processor. Beat eggs, then combine with salt and corn. Pour into a casserole and bake uncovered in a preheated 350° oven for 35 to 40 minutes.

To prepare ahead of time: This can be baked in the morning; underbake slightly, then finish baking shortly before serving.

Green Peppers with Cream

(serves about 4)

4 cups sliced green peppers
2 tablespoons butter
salt and pepper to taste
1 teaspoon dried oregano
1/2 cup heavy whipping cream

Soak oregano in the cream. Sauté sliced peppers in the butter for 1 or 2 minutes, seasoning with salt and pepper. Add cream and oregano and simmer for 1 or 2 minutes; peppers should remain crisp. Serve at once.

To prepare ahead of time: Peppers can be sliced 1 day ahead; refrigerate in a tightly sealed plastic bag. Bring to room temperature 2 hours before serving, then proceed with the cooking.

Green, red, and yellow sweet peppers

(*serves 6 to 8*)

3 large green peppers
3 large red peppers
3 or 4 yellow peppers
1/4 cup butter (1/2 stick)
salt and pepper to taste

Peel green and red peppers with a potato peeler, removing as much of the skin as possible. Cut all the peppers in strips about 1/4-inch wide. Heat butter, add sliced peppers, then toss and cook for 1 or 2 minutes. Season and serve. Do not overcook; they must be cooked quickly, like Chinese stir-fry.

To prepare ahead of time: Peppers can be sliced 1 day ahead; refrigerate in a tightly sealed plastic bag. Bring to room temperature 2 hours before serving, then proceed with the cooking.

Spinach Quiche, Greek Style

(serves 8 to 10)

- 2 (10-ounce) packages frozen chopped spinach
- 2 large onions, finely chopped
- 2 garlic cloves, mashed (or 2 teaspoons from *garlic oil*, page 28)
- 1/3 cup olive oil (or any good vegetable oil)
- 1/2 cup finely chopped fresh parsley
- 1/3 cup finely chopped fresh mint
- 2 teaspoons salt
- 1/2 teaspoon pepper
- 1/4 teaspoon rosemary
- 1/2 teaspoon basil
- 1/2 teaspoon oregano
- 1/3 cup uncooked rice
- 3 large eggs
- 1/8 pound grated parmesan cheese (about 1/2 cup grated)

Defrost spinach, drain, then chop again in a food processor. Sauté onions and garlic in the oil for about 5 minutes, stirring frequently. Add parsley, mint, salt, pepper, rosemary, basil, and oregano, and continue to cook another minute or so. Stir in chopped spinach and remove from heat. Beat eggs, then add rice, spinach mixture, and grated cheese. Pour into a greased 10-inch quiche dish; cover with foil and bake in a preheated 350° oven for 50 minutes. Remove foil and continue baking another 10 minutes.

To prepare ahead of time: This can be made 1 day before. Cover and refrigerate. Bring to room temperature, then reheat in a 350° oven. This freezes, too; defrost completely, then reheat in a 350° oven.

Spinach Phyllo Strudel

(*serves 10 to 12*)

1 large onion, chopped
2 (10-ounce) packages frozen chopped spinach, thawed and drained
2 tablespoons butter
3 eggs, slightly beaten
1/2 pound feta cheese
6 ounces farmers cheese or pot cheese
1/4 cup chopped fresh parsley
2 tablespoons chopped fresh dill
1 cup chopped green onions
salt and pepper to taste
1/4 teaspoon nutmeg
1/2 pound phyllo pastry sheets (about 14 to 16 sheets)
1/2 pound melted butter (best if *clarified*, page 28)
1 cup dry bread crumbs

Sauté onion in the 2 tablespoons butter until tender and lightly browned. Add spinach and cook for 1 minute. Whirl feta and pot cheese in a food processor, then add them to spinach, together with eggs, parsley, dill, green onions, salt, pepper, and nutmeg. Cook and stir over moderate heat for 2 minutes. Remove from heat and cool.

Using the phyllo sheets, prepare to make 2 rolls. For each, place 1 phyllo sheet on a board and brush with butter and sprinkle with crumbs. (Cover remaining phyllo, first with waxed paper and then with a damp towel, to prevent drying and crumbling.) Repeat with more phyllo, butter, and crumbs until you have a total of 6 to 8 sheets. Place half the spinach mixture along the longest side and roll up jelly-roll style. Lift roll, using spatulas, and place seam-side down in a lightly greased baking pan with sides. Repeat process with phyllo and spinach to make a second roll. Bake them in a preheated 375° oven for 15 minutes, then remove from oven and cut halfway through the rolls into 2-inch lengths. Return to oven, reduce heat to 350°, and bake another 20 to 30 minutes—until well browned. Finish slicing and serve either hot or warm.

To prepare ahead of time: The rolls can be assembled 1 day ahead; bake before serving. They freeze well, too (best done *before* baking); defrost for 1 hour, then proceed with the baking. If frozen the baking will take longer.

Potatoes Anna in Nonstick Skillets

(*serves 10 to 12*)

    8 large baking potatoes
    salt and pepper
    1 cup melted butter (2 sticks)

You will need 2 nonstick skillets, 9 or 10 inches in diameter. Remove the plastic handles from the skillets, because they will not take intense oven heat. Peel potatoes and slice thin. Cover bottom of skillets with a little butter, then arrange sliced potatoes in a decorative flower pattern (only the bottom layer need be arranged). Season with salt and pepper and spoon melted butter over the layer. Continue layering potatoes in the same way, ending with melted butter. Bake uncovered in a preheated 425° oven for 1 1/2 hours or possibly longer—until very well browned. Drain off excess butter, then turn out upside down on oven-proof dishes or platters. Shortly before serving, return to a 425° oven for as long as is needed to heat the potatoes to burning hot.

To prepare ahead of time: These can be prepared in the morning; leave them at room temperature, lightly covered. Reheat as directed shortly before serving.

Potato pancakes

(makes about 24 potato pancakes)

4 large baking potatoes
2 teaspoons salt
pinch of pepper
4 eggs
1/4 cup flour
vegetable oil

Peel potatoes, then grate them by hand; or, if you have a food processor, grate them with the grating disk, then insert the metal knife and pulse on and off to chop. Remove from processor bowl, drain off some of the liquid, and add remaining ingredients. *Note*: You need about 4 cups grated potatoes.

In a heavy skillet, add vegetable oil to about 1/4-inch depth and heat to moderately hot. Drop potato pancakes by spoonfuls into skillet and cook until well browned on both sides. Drain on paper towels. Shortly before serving, place pancakes in a large flat roasting pan in a single layer and heat in a preheated 400° oven until piping hot.

To prepare ahead of time: These can be cooked 1 day ahead; cover and keep refrigerated. Remove from refrigerator 2 hours ahead of serving, then follow instructions for oven heating. They freeze well too; freeze them between layers of plastic wrap. Defrost to use, then reheat as directed.

French Fried Potato Baskets

(*makes 12*)

10 large baking potatoes, peeled
vegetable oil
salt

Use the special gadget known as a French potato-basket fryer for these. Plan to make 1 potato basket at a time. Shred one potato on a shredding disk with 1/8-inch holes. Dip both parts of the potato-basket fryer in hot vegetable oil heated to 375° in a deep fat fryer, then line the larger part of the basket with shredded potatoes. Fit smaller basket on top and clamp together. Fry in the hot oil until well browned. Remove, drain, unfasten, and remove basket. If potatoes stick, hit basket firmly on the table. Continue making the other potato baskets, remembering to dip both parts of the basket-fryer in hot oil before filling each time. When all the potatoes have been cooked, sprinkle them generously with salt. Just before serving, place potato baskets on a large baking pan and reheat uncovered in a preheated 400° oven for about 5 minutes. Watch that they do not burn.

To prepare ahead of time: These can be made in the morning; leave at room temperature, then reheat as directed. They are quite good after freezing, but not as delicious as when made and eaten the same day. To freeze, place in plastic bags and seal.

Potatoes, Onions, and Cheese

(*serves 6 to 8*)

4 medium-size potatoes
2 onions
1/2 pound jack cheese (or cheddar)
salt and pepper to taste
2 cups milk
1 cup heavy whipping cream

Slice potatoes, onions, and cheese. Layer them in a large, shallow casserole, seasoning them as you proceed. Pour milk over all and bake uncovered in a preheated 350° oven for 1 hour and 15 minutes. Remove from oven and set aside until about 1 hour before serving. Pour cream over the top and return to a 350° oven and bake until potatoes are fully cooked and top is browned (1 to 1 1/2 hours longer).

To prepare ahead of time: This can be prepared 1 day ahead; cover and refrigerate. Bring to room temperature, then reheat in a 350° oven. This freezes well. To serve, defrost completely, then reheat in a 350° oven.

Zucchini Stuffed with Spinach

(*serves 4 to 8*)

4 medium-size zucchini
1 (10-ounce) package frozen chopped spinach
2 tablespoons butter
2 tablespoons flour
1/2 cup milk
1/2 teaspoon salt
1/4 teaspoon pepper
1/8 teaspoon nutmeg
1/2 cup grated imported swiss cheese
2 tablespoons dry bread crumbs
2 tablespoons grated parmesan cheese

Wash zucchini and trim ends. Boil in lightly salted water for 3 minutes, then drain well. Cut zucchini in half lengthwise and scoop out seeds. Place halves upside down on paper towels to drain more.

Defrost spinach and drain thoroughly. Melt butter in a skillet and add flour. Remove from heat, then add milk, stirring well. Return to heat and stir until mixture boils, then add salt, pepper, and nutmeg. Simmer 2 minutes and add spinach; simmer another minute. Remove from heat and add swiss cheese. Cool, then fill zucchini halves with spinach mixture. Combine bread crumbs and parmesan and sprinkle over the filled zucchini. Place on the upper shelf of a preheated 350° oven and bake until very hot—15 to 20 minutes.

To prepare ahead of time: This can be prepared 1 day ahead, up to the point of the final baking; cover and refrigerate. Bring to room temperature 2 hours before serving, then proceed with the final baking.

Salads and salad dressings

Avocado, Tomato, and Honeydew Melon Salad

>   avocados, peeled and cut in 1/2-inch cubes
>   tomatoes, peeled and cut in 1/2-inch cubes
>   honeydew melon, peeled, seeded, and cut in 1/2-inch cubes
>   *vinaigrette* (page 152)
>   boston lettuce

Combine equal amounts of avocado, tomato, and melon. Cover with vinaigrette and refrigerate. When ready to serve, spoon salad onto lettuce leaves with some of the vinaigrette.

To prepare ahead of time: This can be prepared in the morning; keep covered and refrigerated.

Red Cabbage, Raisin, and Onion Slaw

(serves about 4)

>   4 cups sliced or shredded red cabbage
>   1 small onion, thinly sliced or chopped
>   1/3 cup raisins, soaked in hot water, then drained
>   *vinaigrette* (page 152)
>   salt and pepper to taste

Combine cabbage, onion, and raisins, then add vinaigrette, salt, and pepper to taste. Cover and chill.

To prepare ahead of time: This can be prepared 3 days ahead; keep covered and refrigerated.

Cantaloupe, Red Pepper, and Romaine Salad

(*serves 4*)

1/2 cantaloupe, peeled and seeded, then cut in cubes
1 small sweet red pepper, cut in thin strips
1/2 head of romaine lettuce
2 green onions, chopped
1 tablespoon finely chopped fresh dill
vinaigrette (page 152)

Combine all ingredients except vinaigrette in a salad bowl, then add vinaigrette, toss, and serve.

To prepare ahead of time: Ingredients (except vinaigrette) can be combined in a bowl in the morning; cover tightly with plastic wrap and refrigerate. Add vinaigrette just before serving.

Pickled Beets and Red Onion Salad

1 (1-pound) can sliced pickled beets, drained
1 red onion, sliced
1/2 cup olive oil
1 tablespoon vinegar
salt and pepper to taste

Combine ingredients and cover. Leave at room temperature for several hours, then refrigerate. Serve cold or at room temperature.

To prepare ahead of time: This can be prepared 1 week ahead; keep covered and refrigerated.

Cobb Salad, My Way

(serves 6)

    1 large head of lettuce (or romaine), finely chopped or shredded
    1 1/2 to 2 cups cooked, chopped chicken
    2 large tomatoes, peeled and chopped
    1/2 cup crumbled roquefort cheese
    1 large avocado, peeled and chopped
    3 hard-boiled eggs, finely chopped
    6 green onions, finely chopped
    1/2 pound bacon, cooked and crumbled
    vinaigrette (page 152)

Arrange lettuce in very large soup bowls (or on dinner plates). Carefully arrange the chopped chicken, tomatoes, roquefort cheese, avocado, eggs, green onions, and crumbled bacon on top of each in a decorative pattern. Bring to table and let guests help themselves to the vinaigrette.

To prepare ahead of time: All of the elements of this salad can be prepared in the morning; the bacon and cheese should be left covered at room temperature but the other ingredients should be kept refrigerated in separate bowls.

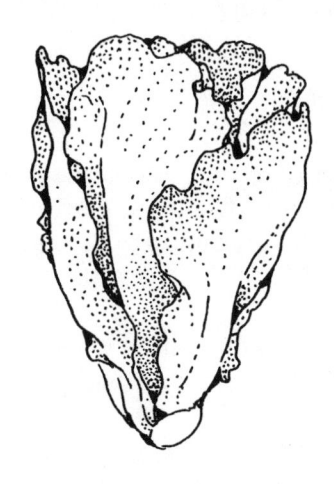

Fennel and Green Grape Salad

(*serves 4 to 6*)

1 large fennel
4 green onions, finely chopped
1 1/2 cups seedless green grapes
sour cream-dill dressing (page 153)

Slice fennel in circles (cut crosswise) and combine with grapes and chopped green onion in a bowl. Cover and chill. Add dressing to taste just before serving.

To prepare ahead of time: Salad can be arranged in a bowl in the morning; cover tightly with plastic wrap and keep refrigerated.

Hearts of Boston Lettuce with an Egg Dressing

(*serves 6*)

6 heads of boston lettuce
4 hard-boiled eggs, chopped
1/2 cup mayonnaise
1/2 cup Durkee's salad dressing
1/4 to 1/3 cup milk

Remove outer leaves of lettuce and place in plastic bags, tightly closed, in the refrigerator. Combine mayonnaise, Durkee's dressing, and eggs, then thin gradually to desired consistency with the milk.

To serve: Place lettuce hearts on individual salad plates, then spoon a generous amount of the egg dressing over each.

To prepare ahead of time: The egg dressing can be made 2 days ahead; keep covered and refrigerated.

Ahead-of-Time Combination Salad

(serves about 8)

2 cups cherry tomatoes, quartered
2 green peppers, coarsely chopped
4 green onions, chopped
2 cups chopped celery
2 cucumbers, peeled, seeded, and chopped
vinaigrette (page 152)
salt and pepper to taste

Combine vegetables in a bowl, then add vinaigrette to taste and season with salt and pepper. Cover and chill at least 8 hours. Serve in small bowls or in tomato shells or avocado halves.

To prepare ahead of time: This can be prepared 2 to 3 days ahead; keep tightly covered and refrigerated. Stir once a day.

Greek Salad with Fennel and Feta

(serves about 10)

1 large fennel, sliced
3 cups thinly sliced cucumbers
1 red onion, thinly sliced
5 or 6 tomatoes, cut in small wedges
2 large green peppers, sliced
2 tablespoons finely chopped fresh dill
2 cups diced feta cheese
vinaigrette (page 152)

Combine all vegetables in a large salad bowl and sprinkle with chopped dill. Scatter diced feta on the salad, then add vinaigrette to taste, toss and serve.

To prepare ahead of time: The salad can be assembled in the morning. Cover tightly with plastic wrap and refrigerate; add vinaigrette just before serving.

Romaine and Bean Sprout Salad

(*serves 4 to 6*)

1 medium-size romaine lettuce
3 cups bean sprouts
3 tomatoes, cut in small wedges
3 green onions, finely chopped
1/4 pound bacon, cooked and crumbled
vinaigrette (page 152)

Wash and drain romaine and bean sprouts, then dry them on paper towels. Chill thoroughly. Place romaine (cut or torn into bite-size pieces) in a salad bowl and add bean sprouts, tomatoes, and green onion. Cover tightly with plastic wrap; keep chilled until time to serve. Just before serving, sprinkle salad with bacon, add vinaigrette to taste, toss and serve.

To prepare ahead of time: Salad can be assembled in the morning (without bacon or vinaigrette), covered and refrigerated until time to serve. Bacon can be cooked and crumbled in the morning; cover and leave at room temperature.

Spinach, Romaine, and Almond Salad

(*serves about 8*)

1 large romaine lettuce
2 bunches of fresh spinach, washed and stems removed
1/2 pound bacon, cooked and crumbled
1 cup sliced almonds, toasted

for dressing

2 tablespoons finely chopped or grated onion
1/2 teaspoon salt
1/2 teaspoon dry mustard
1 1/2 tablespoons sugar
1/4 cup white wine vinegar
1 cup salad oil

Making the dressing: Combine onion, salt, mustard, sugar, and vinegar and stir until sugar has dissolved. Gradually whisk in the oil. Refrigerate in a jar with a tight-fitting cover.

Making the salad: Combine spinach and romaine—torn into bite-size pieces—in a large salad bowl. Scatter toasted sliced almonds over the greens. Just before serving, add bacon and dressing, toss and serve.

To prepare ahead of time: The dressing can be made 1 week ahead if kept tightly covered and refrigerated. The bacon can be cooked in the morning; cover and leave at room temperature. The almonds can be toasted in the morning. The salad greens can be arranged in a bowl, covered tightly with plastic wrap and refrigerated.

Spinach and Orange Salad

(*serves about 12*)

3 bunches fresh spinach, washed and stems removed
4 navel oranges
1/2 pound bacon, cooked and crumbled
1/4 cup sesame seeds, lightly toasted in a 350° oven

for dressing

    1 1/2 tablespoons sugar
    2 tablespoons finely chopped (or grated) onion
    1/2 teaspoon salt
    3/4 teaspoon dry mustard
    1/4 cup white wine vinegar
    1 cup salad oil

Making the dressing: Combine ingredients and whisk together, then store covered in the refrigerator.

Making the salad: Peel oranges and carefully remove segments, discarding white pith. Place spinach in a large salad bowl and sprinkle with crumbled bacon and toasted sesame seeds. Scatter orange segments over the top. Just before serving, add dressing, toss and serve.

To prepare ahead of time: The dressing can be made 5 days ahead; keep tightly covered and refrigerated. Bacon and sesame seeds can be prepared in the morning; leave them at room temperature. Orange segments can be readied in the morning too; keep refrigerated.

Chicken Salad in Cantaloupe with Ginger Dressing

(serves 8)

4 ripe cantaloupes, halved and seeds removed
4 cups diced cooked chicken
3/4 cup chopped green pepper
1 1/2 cups finely chopped celery

for dressing

>6 tablespoons chopped preserved ginger
>3 tablespoons syrup from preserved ginger
>grated rind of 2 lemons
>1/4 cup lemon juice
>1 cup mayonnaise
>1 cup sour cream
>1/2 teaspoon salt

for garnish

>canned mandarin orange segments
>1 cup macadamia nuts

Combine ingredients for the dressing, then chill. Combine chicken, green pepper, and celery and chill. When ready to serve, fill cantaloupe halves with chicken mixture and spoon on a generous amount of dressing. Garnish with mandarin orange segments and macadamia nuts.

To prepare ahead of time: The dressing can be prepared 3 days ahead; keep covered and refrigerated. The chicken can be combined with the vegetables 1 day before and kept refrigerated. The cantaloupe halves can be filled in the morning; cover and refrigerate them. Shortly before serving, add the dressing and garnish.

Green Goddess Seafood Salad

(*serves 6*)

1 1/2 pounds cooked seafood (choice of, or mixture of, cooked shrimp, crabmeat, lobster)
7 hard-boiled eggs
8 artichoke hearts (canned)
2 tablespoons lemon juice
cucumber slices
green and red pepper slices
lettuce leaves

for green goddess dressing

>1 garlic clove, mashed (or 1 teaspoon garlic from *garlic oil*, page 28)
>6 anchovies (drained of oil)
>8 green onions
>1/2 cup fresh parsley
>2 tablespoons lemon juice
>1 tablespoon white wine vinegar
>1/4 teaspoon tarragon
>1/2 teaspoon salt
>1/4 teaspoon pepper
>1 cup mayonnaise
>1 cup sour cream

Making the green goddess dressing: A food processor or blender makes short work of this. Whirl together all ingredients except mayonnaise and sour cream until puréed. Fold in mayonnaise and sour cream. Cover and chill.

To assemble: Cut seafood into bite-size pieces. Cut eggs into wedges. Combine seafood and eggs in a bowl. Season if needed and sprinkle with the 2 tablespoons lemon juice. Arrange on lettuce leaves and surround with artichoke hearts and cucumber and pepper slices. Serve with the green goddess dressing; or pour dressing on seafood first and toss to combine, then arrange on lettuce leaves.

To prepare ahead of time: Green goddess dressing can be prepared 3 days ahead; keep covered and refrigerated.

Russian Buffet Salad

(serves about 16)

for salad

    2 cups finely chopped celery
    2 cups cooked, diced carrots
    2 cups cooked, diced green beans
    2 cups cooked, diced potatoes
    2 cups cooked green peas
    2 cups diced cucumber
    3 tablespoons lemon juice
    3 tablespoons anchovy paste
    2 or more cups mayonnaise

for garnish

    large, cooked shrimp (32 or more)
    thinly sliced ham (32 or more slices)
    smoked salmon slices (optional)
    8 or more hard-boiled eggs, cut in wedges
    pickled beet slices
    pimento-stuffed olives
    ripe olives
    tomato slices or wedges
    fresh parsley

Preparing the salad: Combine all vegetables in a large bowl. Mix together anchovy paste, lemon juice, and mayonnaise, then stir into the vegetables, adding more mayonnaise as needed to moisten well. Taste for seasoning, then cover and chill.

To assemble: Place the salad on a large platter and form into a mound. Arrange all the ingredients listed for the garnish on and around the mound of salad.

To prepare ahead of time: The salad can be mixed 1 or 2 days ahead; keep tightly covered and refrigerated.

Vinaigrette

(makes 3 1/2 cups)

1 tablespoon salt
1/2 teaspoon black pepper
1 teaspoon dry mustard
2 teaspoons sugar (optional)
1 garlic clove, mashed (or 1 teaspoon garlic from *garlic oil*, page 28)
1 scant cup vinegar (or part lemon juice)
2 cups salad oil (can use all or part olive oil)

Combine salt, black pepper, mustard, sugar, garlic, and vinegar. Beat together thoroughly, then gradually whisk in the oil. Store in a tightly sealed jar (or in several jars) in the refrigerator. Bring to room temperature before using.

To prepare ahead of time: This can be prepared 2 to 3 weeks ahead, but it must be kept tightly covered and refrigerated. Be sure to bring it to room temperature before using.

Sour Cream–Dill Dressing

(makes about 1 quart)

3 cups sour cream
1 1/2 teaspoons salt
1/2 teaspoon pepper
4 green onions, finely chopped
1/2 to 3/4 cup finely chopped fresh dill
1/4 cup white wine vinegar

Whisk ingredients together, then spoon into a large jar with a tight-fitting cover and refrigerate.

To prepare ahead of time: This can be prepared 1 week ahead; keep covered and refrigerated.

Russian Dressing

(makes about 1 1/2 cups)

1 cup mayonnaise
1/4 cup ketchup
1/4 cup chili sauce
2 teaspoons dijon-style mustard
2 teaspoons grated horseradish
1 teaspoon Worcestershire sauce
2 to 3 teaspoons red wine vinegar
dash of Tabasco sauce

Whisk all ingredients together. Store, covered, in the refrigerator.

To prepare ahead of time: This can be prepared 2 weeks ahead; keep tightly covered and refrigerated.

Green Mayonnaise

(makes about 1 quart)

1 whole egg
3 egg yolks
1 1/2 teaspoons salt
1 1/2 teaspoons sugar
1 1/2 teaspoons dry mustard
1/2 teaspoon paprika
1/4 teaspoon pepper
1/4 to 1/2 teaspoon tarragon
1/4 cup chopped fresh dill
3/4 cup chopped fresh parsley
4 or 5 green onions, chopped
1/3 cup white wine vinegar
2 1/2 cups salad oil, preferably all or part olive oil

Combine all ingredients except oil in the bowl of a food processor and whirl together until everything is finely chopped and well mixed. Start adding the oil very slowly—a few drops at a time—then gradually add the rest of the oil. Store well covered in glass jars in the refrigerator.

To prepare ahead of time: This can be made up to 10 days ahead, but must be kept tightly covered and refrigerated.

Breads, rolls, and coffeecakes

CRISP WATER ROLLS

(makes 2 dozen)

    2 packages dry yeast
    1/2 cup warm water
    2 tablespoons sugar
    1 1/2 cups lukewarm water
    1 tablespoon salt
    2 tablespoons melted butter
    4 egg whites, slightly beaten
    6 1/4 cups sifted flour (28 1/4 ounces)
    cornmeal

Dissolve yeast in the warm water, then stir in the sugar. Place the lukewarm water, salt, butter, and egg whites in a large bowl. Stir in dissolved yeast, then gradually beat in the flour with an electric dough hook or beat in part of the flour with a wooden spoon and knead in the rest with your hands. Dough should become smooth and blistered. Cover and let rise for about 1 hour—until doubled in bulk.

Turn out on a floured board and knead for half a minute, then divide dough into 4 parts. Cut each into 6 portions and shape these into rounds. Let them rest for 3 minutes, then shape into ovals and place on greased baking pans which have been sprinkled generously with cornmeal. Let rise 20 to 30 minutes. Brush tops with ice water and bake at 425° for 15 minutes. Brush again with ice water, reduce oven to 300°, and bake about 10 minutes longer.

To prepare ahead of time: These can be baked 1 day ahead. Reheat before serving. These rolls freeze well; reheat before serving.

French Crusty Rye Bread

(*makes 2 to 4 loaves*)

2 packages dry yeast
2/3 cup warm water
1 tablespoon sugar
1 tablespoon salt
2 cups lukewarm water
2 1/2 cups rye flour (spoon lightly to measure)
6 cups sifted white flour (27 ounces)
3 tablespoons caraway seeds
1 egg white mixed with 1 tablespoon water
Kosher-style salt
cornmeal

Dissolve yeast in the 2/3 cup warm water, then stir in sugar and salt. Place lukewarm water in a large bowl and add dissolved yeast. Beat in the rye flour and as much of the white flour as needed to make a stiff dough. Turn out on a floured board and knead thoroughly, adding more white flour as needed. Beat in (if using a dough hook), or knead in the caraway seeds. Place dough in a greased bowl and cover. Let rise until doubled in bulk—45 minutes or longer; then punch down and turn out on a floured board. Divide into 2 to 4 portions and let them "relax" for 5 minutes. Shape into long loaves and place on well-greased baking tins that have been heavily sprinkled with cornmeal. Score tops of loaves and brush with egg white. Let rise about 30 minutes, brush again with egg white, and sprinkle with salt. Bake in a preheated 400° oven for 30 minutes. Reduce heat to 300° and bake another 20 to 25 minutes. Remove breads from pans and cool on racks.

To prepare ahead of time: These can be baked 1 day ahead; wrap in foil and refrigerate. Reheat uncovered before serving. Like most breads, this freezes well. Defrost, then reheat uncovered.

Cornmeal Yeast Bread

(*makes 2 or 3 loaves*)

2 packages dry yeast
1/2 cup warm water
1 teaspoon sugar
1 3/4 cups milk
1/3 cup melted butter
1/3 cup sugar
4 teaspoons salt
2 eggs
1 2/3 cups yellow cornmeal
6 1/2 cups sifted flour (29 ounces)
4 tablespoons additional yellow cornmeal

Dissolve yeast in warm water and sprinkle with the 1 teaspoon sugar. Combine milk, butter, 1/3 cup sugar, salt, and eggs and beat well, then stir in dissolved yeast. Beat in the cornmeal and as much flour as possible. Turn out on a floured board and knead in whatever flour you were not able to beat in. Place in a greased bowl and cover. Let rise until doubled in bulk—40 to 60 minutes. Divide into 2 or 3 portions; place in greased loaf pans, brush tops with cold water, and sprinkle generously with the additional cornmeal. Let rise until doubled (30 to 45 minutes), then bake in a preheated 350° oven for about 45 minutes or until well browned and done: breads will have a hollow sound when tapped. Remove breads from pans and cool on racks.

To prepare ahead of time: These can be baked 1 day ahead, but do not overbake. Wrap well and refrigerate. To serve, bring to room temperature, then reheat wrapped in foil. These breads freeze well too; follow the same instructions as for day-ahead preparation.

Butter Rolls

(makes 32 rolls)

1 package dry yeast
1/4 cup warm water
1 tablespoon sugar
3/4 cup milk
1/2 cup sugar
3 eggs, beaten
1 cup melted butter (2 sticks)
4 1/2 cups sifted flour (20 1/4 ounces)
1/2 teaspoon salt
cold milk

Dissolve yeast in warm water and sprinkle with 1 tablespoon sugar. Combine milk, 1/2 cup sugar, eggs, and 1/2 cup melted butter in a large bowl, then add dissolved yeast and stir. Beat in flour and salt. Cover with a damp cloth and let rise 2 to 2 1/2 hours or until doubled in bulk.

Divide dough into 2 parts. Roll out each one on a floured board into a large circle about 1/4-inch thick. Spread each with 1/4 cup melted butter. Cut into 16 wedges and roll them up from the wide ends to the tips. Place on greased baking pans with tip ends down. Let rise again until doubled—2 to 2 1/2 hours. Brush with cold milk and bake in a preheated 400° oven for about 12 minutes. Serve hot.

To prepare ahead of time: These can be baked 1 day before; wrap well and refrigerate. Reheat before serving. These freeze well, but underbake them slightly. To serve, defrost, then bake at 400° until browned and very hot.

Heavenly Brioche

(*makes 12 to 16*)

1 1/2 packages dry yeast
1/3 cup warm water
1/3 cup milk
1/2 pound butter (2 sticks), melted and cooled
1/2 cup sugar
1 teaspoon salt
4 whole eggs
4 egg yolks
5 cups sifted flour (22 1/2 ounces)
1 egg, slightly beaten with 1 tablespoon water

Dissolve yeast in warm water. Combine milk, butter, sugar, salt, eggs, and egg yolks in a large bowl and beat well. Add dissolved yeast. Add flour and beat thoroughly either with an electric dough hook or with a wooden spoon. Place in a greased bowl, cover, and let rise from 45 minutes to 1 1/2 hours—until doubled in bulk. Knock down the dough, cover, and refrigerate at least 3 hours, or better, overnight. If dough seems to rise in the refrigerator too quickly, press it down.

Turn dough out on a floured board. Grease muffin tins or brioche pans. Take small pieces of dough and form into balls that will fill muffin tins or brioche pans 1/3 to 1/2 full. Make an indentation in the top center of each, then make smaller balls of dough and place them in those indentations, pressing them firmly in place. Let them rise about 45 minutes, brush with beaten egg, and bake in a preheated 400° oven for approximately 15 minutes.

To prepare ahead of time: These can be baked 2 days ahead; keep well wrapped and refrigerated. Reheat before serving. They freeze well, too; reheat before serving.

Honey-Walnut Rolls

(*makes 24*)

2 packages dry yeast
1/2 cup warm water
1 tablespoon sugar
2 eggs
1/4 cup melted butter (1/2 stick)
1/2 cup milk
1/2 teaspoon salt
1/2 cup sugar
4 cups sifted flour (18 ounces)
1 1/2 cups walnuts, lightly toasted, then chopped

for honey-butter

    1/2 pound butter (2 sticks), room temperature
    1 1/3 cups honey
    2/3 cup brown sugar (pack to measure)

Preparing honey-butter: Beat ingredients together, then chill briefly; it should be cool but not too hard.

Dissolve yeast in warm water and stir in the 1 tablespoon of sugar. Beat eggs, melted butter, milk, salt, and 1/2 cup sugar together in a large bowl. Add dissolved yeast and beat in flour. Place in a greased bowl, cover, and let rise until doubled in bulk—45 minutes to 1 hour.

Divide dough in half and roll each portion into a rectangle 9 by 15 inches. Spread 1 portion with 1/4 cup honey-butter and fold in thirds. Turn dough so open ends face you. Roll out again (to same dimensions) and spread with another 1/4 cup honey-butter. Sprinkle with half the chopped walnuts, then roll up jelly-roll fashion and cut in 12 pieces. Repeat process with the other portion of dough. Spread remaining honey-butter in a 9- by 14-inch pan and place the 24 pieces cut sides down in the pan. Let rise 25 to 30 minutes, then bake in a preheated 375° oven for 30 to 35 minutes or until well browned. Remove from oven and cool 3 to 5 minutes, then turn out upside down on greased foil. Serve warm.

To prepare ahead of time: These can be baked 2 days ahead; keep covered and refrigerated. Reheat before serving. They freeze well; to serve, defrost, then wrap in foil and reheat before serving.

Popovers guaranteed

(*makes 6*)

    1 cup sifted flour (4 1/2 ounces)
    3/4 teaspoon salt
    1 cup milk (room temperature)
    2 eggs (room temperature)
    1 teaspoon oil

Combine flour and salt in a bowl. Beat eggs slightly, then add to flour alternately with the milk and oil, beating only until mixture is smooth. Cover and set aside for 1 hour or longer. Grease Pyrex custard cups with vegetable shortening, then pour in batter 1/2 to 2/3 full. Put cups on a baking sheet and place in a cold oven. Yes, a cold oven! Immediately turn oven to 400° and bake 45 to 60 minutes, until well puffed and browned.

To prepare ahead of time: The batter can be made the day before or in the morning; cover and refrigerate. Bring batter to room temperature before filling cups and check its thickness: it should be about the consistency of very heavy cream. If too thick, add a tablespoon or so of milk and stir well.

Family-Style Cinnamon Rolls

(*makes about 2 dozen*)

2 packages dry yeast
1/3 cup warm water
1/2 cup melted butter (1 stick)
1/2 teaspoon salt
2/3 cup milk
2/3 cup sugar
3 cold eggs
4 1/2 cups sifted flour (20 1/4 ounces)
more melted butter
1/2 cup sugar
2 tablespoons cinnamon
1 cup raisins

for the icing

2 tablespoons butter
3 tablespoons milk
sifted powdered sugar
1 1/2 teaspoons vanilla
sliced toasted almonds

Preparing the yeast dough: Dissolve yeast in the warm water. Combine melted butter, salt, and milk. Beat eggs and add them to the butter-milk mixture, then stir in the dissolved yeast. Beat in the flour. Place dough in a greased bowl, cover and let rise until doubled in bulk, 1 hour or longer.

Making the rolls: Turn dough out on a floured board and divide in half. Roll out each part to 1/4-inch thickness and spread with melted butter. Combine the 1/2 cup sugar and cinnamon and sprinkle half on each portion; scatter with raisins. Roll up jelly-roll style, then cut each roll in 12 pieces. Place slices cut sides down in 2 well-greased 9-inch round (or 9-inch square) metal pans. Let rise about 30 minutes, then bake in a preheated 350° oven for about 40 minutes. Remove from oven and place on a rack to cool briefly, then cover top of each with icing.

Making the icing: Melt the 2 tablespoons butter and add milk, then remove from heat. Add sifted powdered sugar, stirring, until of spreading consistency. Stir in vanilla. Spread on the rolls as directed above and immediately sprinkle generously with sliced toasted almonds.

To prepare ahead of time: These can be baked 2 days ahead; keep covered and refrigerated. Reheat before serving. They keep well frozen; to serve, defrost and reheat before serving.

Walnut Coffeecake

(*makes 2 cakes*)

1 package dry yeast
1/4 cup warm water
1 cup milk
3 egg yolks
1/2 cup melted butter (1 stick)
1/4 cup sugar
1/2 teaspoon salt
4 cups sifted flour (18 ounces)

for filling

> 3 egg whites
> 1 cup sugar
> 2 cups walnuts, lightly toasted, then finely chopped
> 2 teaspoons cinnamon

for icing

> 2 tablespoons melted butter
> 2 tablespoons milk
> sifted powdered sugar
> 1 teaspoon vanilla

Dissolve yeast in the warm water. In a large mixing bowl combine milk, egg yolks, melted butter, sugar, and salt and beat slightly. When this is warm to the touch, add dissolved yeast and stir well. Gradually beat in the flour. Cover and refrigerate overnight.

Making the filling: Beat egg whites until almost stiff, then gradually beat in the 1 cup of sugar. Combine chopped walnuts and cinnamon and fold into the egg white mixture.

Making the icing: Combine melted butter and milk, then gradually stir in sifted powdered sugar until of spreading consistency. Add vanilla and set aside.

Making the coffeecakes: Divide dough into 2 portions. Roll out each into a rectangle 9 by 12 inches. Cover each with half the filling, then roll up like jelly rolls. Place them on greased baking pans and form each into a horseshoe shape. If desired, brush tops with a little cold milk. Let rise until almost double in bulk—about 45 minutes. Bake in a preheated 350° oven for 35 to 45 minutes. Remove from oven and cool, but frost with the icing while cakes are still warm.

To prepare ahead of time: These can be baked 2 days ahead; keep well wrapped and refrigerated. They freeze well too. In either case, reheat before serving.

Danish Pastry Pecan Rolls

(*makes about 40*)

1 pound butter
1/3 cup sifted flour (1 1/2 ounces)
2 packages dry yeast
1/2 cup warm water
1 cup eggs (4 or 5)
1/3 cup sugar
1/2 cup milk
1 teaspoon salt
2 tablespoons honey
1/4 teaspoon mace
1/4 teaspoon cinnamon
1 teaspoon vanilla
1 teaspoon lemon extract
3 3/4 cups sifted flour (1 pound)
1 3/4 cups sifted cake flour (6 ounces)
whole pecans
1 egg beaten with 1 tablespoon water

for filling

    2 cups chopped pecans
    1 cup sugar mixed with 4 tablespoons cinnamon

for syrup

    3/4 pound butter, melted
    1 pound brown sugar
    1/4 cup water

Preparing the dough: Mix the 1 pound of butter and 1/3 cup sifted flour to a paste, either with a wooden spoon or with an electric dough hook. Spread in a 9-inch foil pan and chill 20 minutes. This is the butter-paste.

Dissolve yeast in warm water. Beat eggs with the sugar, milk, salt, honey, mace, cinnamon, vanilla, and lemon extract. Add dissolved yeast. Gradually beat in both kinds of flour. Turn into a floured pan and chill 20 minutes. This is the flour-dough.

Roll out flour-dough into a rectangle 12 by 18 inches and mark in thirds. Place half of the butter-paste in the center. Fold one third of the flour-dough over this, then spread remaining half of butter-paste on the top and fold remaining third of flour-dough over this. Turn dough so that open ends face you, then roll out again, this time into a rectangle 18 by 24 inches. Fold both ends to the middle, then close like a book. Turn dough again so that ends face you and repeat this last step—that is, rolling out, then folding in fourths. Wrap in waxed paper and chill for 30 to 45 minutes.

Remove dough from refrigerator and roll again into a rectangle 18 by 24 inches and again fold in fourths as before. Turn pastry around so that open ends face you, and this time roll into a rectangle about 12 by 30 inches and fold in thirds. Wrap well in waxed paper and chill overnight. If dough appears to rise too quickly, press it down firmly with your hands.

Making the syrup: Combine ingredients in a saucepan and bring slowly to a boil, stirring to dissolve sugar. Simmer 2 minutes, then cool slightly.

Preparing pecan rolls: Spoon syrup into muffin tins, then press pecan halves into syrup. Divide dough into 4 parts. Roll each portion out and spread with beaten egg, then cover thickly with cinnamon-sugar and chopped pecans. Roll up and cut each roll into 10 slices. Place slices cut sides down in the muffin tins. Brush with beaten egg, let rise until slightly puffy, and bake in a preheated 375° oven for 15 to 20 minutes. Turn out upside down on greased foil.

To prepare ahead of time: These can be baked 1 day before; wrap in foil and refrigerate. Reheat before serving. They can be baked and frozen, and should keep for several months; defrost and reheat before serving.

Cornbread

(*serves 6 to 8*)

1 cup yellow cornmeal
1 cup sifted flour (4 1/2 ounces)
2 tablespoons sugar
3 teaspoons baking powder
1 teaspoon salt
1 egg
1 cup milk
1/3 cup melted butter (or vegetable oil)

Combine dry ingredients in a large bowl. Beat egg, milk, and melted butter together and add to dry ingredients. Stir only until blended; do not overmix. Pour into a greased 9-inch square pan and bake in a preheated 400° oven for 20 to 25 minutes.

To prepare ahead of time: Although this is best baked and eaten fresh, it is still good when baked 1 day ahead. Reheat covered with foil in a 400° oven. It can also be frozen; defrost, then reheat covered with foil in a 400° oven.

Cakes, cookies, and pastries

Lemon Cake with Lemon Icing

(*makes 1 large cake or 2 smaller ones*)

1/2 pound butter (2 sticks), room temperature
2 cups sugar
3 large eggs (room temperature)
3 cups sifted cake flour (10 1/2 ounces)
1/2 teaspoon baking soda
1/2 teaspoon salt
1 cup buttermilk or sour milk
grated rind of 2 lemons
2 tablespoons lemon juice

for lemon icing

1 pound powdered sugar
1/4 pound soft butter (1 stick)
grated rind of 1 lemon
1/4 to 1/2 cup lemon juice

Making the lemon cake: Cream butter and sugar together until light and fluffy. Beat in eggs. Sift dry ingredients together and add them alternately with the buttermilk (or sour milk), ending with the dry. DO NOT OVERMIX. Stir in lemon rind and juice. Spoon into well-greased and floured pans (either a large, 4-quart bundt pan or 2 pans about 1 1/2-quart size). Bake in a preheated 325° oven for approximately 1 hour and 10 minutes—or until a wooden pick inserted in center comes out dry. Remove from oven and place on a rack to cool for 10 minutes, then invert on a cake rack and frost with the icing you have prepared.

Making the lemon icing: Cream butter and sugar together, then add lemon rind and slowly beat in lemon juice until spreading consistency is achieved. (Can be done in a food processor.)

To prepare ahead of time: This can be baked 2 to 3 days ahead; cover and refrigerate, but bring to room temperature before serving. It freezes well too; defrost at room temperature the night before serving.

Almond-Cinnamon-Meringue Cake

(*serves 12 to 16*)

    7 egg whites (room temperature)
    1 1/4 cups sugar
    1/4 teaspoon salt
    2 teaspoons cinnamon
    1/2 pound blanched almonds, toasted lightly, then ground

Beat whites until barely stiff. Stir sugar, salt, and cinnamon together, then gradually beat into whites. Fold in ground almonds and spread mixture in a greased and floured pan (9 by 13 inches). Bake in a preheated 350° oven for 20 to 25 minutes. Remove from oven and place on a rack for 5 minutes, then invert on waxed paper to finish cooling. Cut into squares to serve.

To prepare ahead of time: This can be baked 1 or 2 days ahead; wrap well in foil and leave at room temperature. It freezes beautifully.

Variation: Divide cake in thirds, then fill and frost (stacking layers) with 1 cup *chocolate icing* (page 187).

Chocolate Genoise Chantilly Cake

(serves about 20)

2 9-inch layers *chocolate genoise* cake (page 186)
chocolate icing (page 187)

for rum syrup

>1/2 cup water
>1/2 cup sugar
>3 tablespoons dark rum

for chocolate chantilly

>8 ounces dark sweet chocolate
>2 1/2 cups heavy whipping cream
>1 teaspoon vanilla

Making the rum syrup: Dissolve sugar in the water over moderate heat, stirring constantly. Remove from heat and cool slightly, then stir in the rum.

Making the chocolate chantilly: Melt the chocolate with 1/2 cup of the cream, stirring constantly. Add vanilla and remove from heat. Set aside to cool; it should be at room temperature. Whip remaining cream until stiff, then fold in the melted chocolate.

To assemble: Cut each genoise layer in half horizontally, thus producing 4 layers. Place 1 layer on a serving dish and brush or spoon on about 1/4 of the rum syrup. Spread with 1/3 of the chocolate chantilly. Do the same with 2 more cake layers. After placing the fourth layer on top, chill cake thoroughly—if possible in a freezer for several hours. After completely chilled or partially frozen, pour on the chocolate icing, completely covering the cake. If desired, cake can be decorated with chopped pistachios or chocolate leaves.

To prepare ahead of time: This can be completely assembled 1 or 2 days ahead, covered and refrigerated. Or it can be frozen for several months. You can also freeze the cakes, filling, and icing separately; defrost, then assemble as directed.

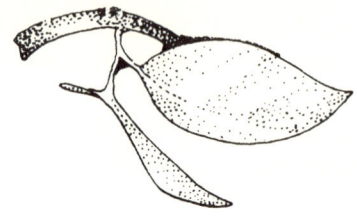

BLACK FOREST TORTE

(*serves 12 to 16*)

2 (9-inch) layers *chocolate genoise* (page 186)
1 (1-pound) can red tart cherries, well drained
maraschino cherries
dark sweet chocolate shavings

for kirsch syrup

> 6 tablespoons sugar
> 1/2 cup water
> 3 tablespoons kirsch

for chocolate filling

> 2 cups heavy whipping cream
> 3/4 cup sugar
> 6 tablespoons (level) unsweetened cocoa (Dutch, preferably)
> 1 teaspoon unflavored gelatin
> 2 tablespoons cold water

Making the kirsch syrup: Combine sugar and water in a small saucepan and stir over moderate heat until sugar has dissolved. Remove from heat and stir in kirsch.

Making the chocolate filling: Chill cream thoroughly. Sift sugar and cocoa together several times. Combine cream with the sugar-cocoa mixture and chill again for 10 minutes. Soak gelatin in the cold water for 5 minutes. Dissolve soaked gelatin over a pan of simmering water. Beat cream mixture until quite thick, then add dissolved gelatin all at once, beating cream at same time.

To assemble: Place 1 layer of chocolate genoise on cake plate. Spoon on half the kirsch syrup. Cover with 1/3 of the chocolate filling and the drained tart cherries. Top with second layer and spoon on remaining syrup. Frost top and sides of cake with remaining filling. Decorate with maraschino cherries and chocolate shavings. Refrigerate (covered with plastic wrap) until time to serve.

To prepare ahead of time: This can be prepared 2 to 3 days before serving; keep covered and refrigerated.

To freeze: The chocolate genoise freezes beautifully. The chocolate filling can be frozen; defrost it overnight in the refrigerator before proceeding.

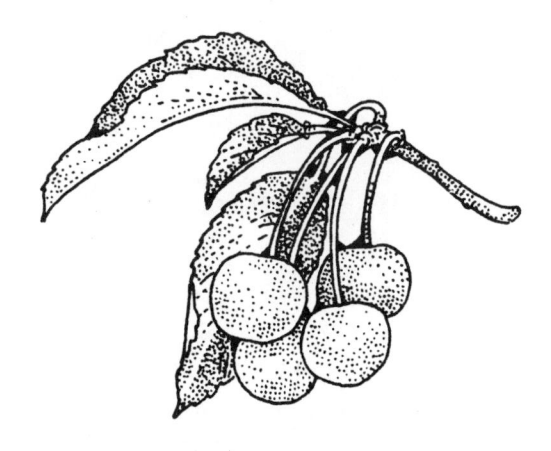

GRAND FINALE CHOCOLATE GÂTEAU

(serves about 20)

1 10-inch *chocolate genoise* cake (page 186)
1 1/2 dozen *almond macaroons* (page 189)
1 cup strawberry jam
1/2 cup Grand Marnier

for chocolate-orange filling

12 ounces dark sweet chocolate
1/4 cup sugar
1/4 cup water
1/8 teaspoon salt
4 egg yolks
1 tablespoon unflavored gelatin
1/4 cup cold water
grated rind of 2 oranges
1 tablespoon Grand Marnier
4 egg whites
2 tablespoons sugar
1 cup heavy whipping cream

for chocolate coating

12 ounces semisweet chocolate
1/4 cup butter (1/2 stick)
1/4 cup light corn syrup

Making the chocolate-orange filling: Combine chocolate, 1/4 cup sugar, 1/4 cup water, and salt in top of double boiler. Stir over simmering water until melted. Beat egg yolks in a bowl, then gradually add melted mixture, and return to top of double boiler. Cook and stir for 3 or 4 minutes. Soak gelatin in the 1/4 cup cold water while mixture is cooking, then add it and stir until dissolved. Remove from heat, add orange rind and Grand Marnier. Cool and stir over ice water until room temperature. Beat egg whites until barely stiff, then beat in the 2 tablespoons of sugar and fold into mixture. Beat cream until stiff and fold cream into mixture too. Chill in refrigerator until ready to assemble.

Making the chocolate coating (see diagram on page 180): Cut 5 pieces of waxed paper each 7 by 8 inches; and cut 1 piece of waxed paper 5 by 17 inches. Place them on lightly greased cookie tins. Melt chocolate, butter, and syrup over simmering water and stir until smooth, then remove from heat and cool to room temperature. Spread 1/2 cup of mixture on the 5 by 17 inch strip of paper and divide remaining coating on the other 5 pieces. Chill until firm—several hours or overnight.

To assemble: Cut chocolate genoise in half horizontally. Place 1 layer in a 10-inch springform pan. Soak macaroons in Grand Marnier. Cover cake layer with half the jam and half the macaroons, then add half the chocolate-orange filling. Place remaining cake layer on top and repeat with macaroons, jam, and remaining filling. Cover and chill for at least 5 hours or overnight. When completely chilled, remove sides of springform but leave bottom of pan in place. Place the gâteau on an attractive serving platter. Remove the 5 small pieces of chocolate coating from refrigerator; as soon as they begin to soften, remove from waxed paper (peels off easily) and place them around the cake, pressing with your hands, folding and pleating at the top as needed. To make a kind of flower topknot, remove long chocolate strip from refrigerator; as soon as it begins to soften, peel off paper and fold in half lengthwise, then roll chocolate loosely into a spiral about 4 inches in diameter. Place on top center of cake and, using your fingers, arrange it to look like a flower. Refrigerate cake until 1 hour before serving. Slice in wedges, leaving the topknot flower in place until the last. *Note*: If chocolate softens too much, return to refrigerator long enough to harden slightly.

To prepare ahead of time: This can be prepared 2 or 3 days ahead; in fact, it should be at least partly prepared 1 day ahead. Keep well covered and refrigerated. The entire gâteau can be frozen; move to refrigerator 2 days before serving to defrost slowly.

GRAND FINALE CHOCOLATE GÂTEAU

Deluxe Pound Cake

(*serves 16 to 20*)

    3/4 pound butter (3 sticks), room temperature
    2 1/4 cups sugar
    8 eggs, room temperature
    grated rind of 1 lemon
    2 tablespoons lemon juice
    2 1/2 teaspoons vanilla
    2 1/4 cups sifted flour
    1/4 teaspoon baking soda
    1/2 teaspoon baking powder
    1/4 teaspoon salt
    1 1/2 teaspoons cream of tartar

Cream butter with 1 1/4 cups of the sugar until very light and fluffy. Separate the eggs and beat in the yolks, reserving the whites for later. Add lemon rind, lemon juice, and vanilla and beat again. Sift flour, baking soda, and baking powder together 3 times, then add to yolk mixture, mixing only until combined. DO NOT OVERMIX. Add salt and cream of tartar to egg whites and beat until frothy, then gradually add remaining 1 cup of sugar and beat until stiff but not dry; fold into the yolk mixture. Pour into a greased and floured bundt or angelfood pan and bake in a preheated 325° oven for 1 1/4 to 1 1/2 hours, or until cake shrinks slightly from pan sides. Turn off oven but leave cake in an additional 10 minutes, then remove and place on a rack for 5 minutes. Invert cake and remove from pan; finish cooling on cake rack.

To prepare ahead of time: This can be baked 2 to 3 days ahead; wrap in double foil and leave at room temperature. This cake freezes very well; defrost overnight at room temperature.

MACADAMIA-PINEAPPLE-RUM CAKE

(*makes 1 large cake or several small ones*)

- 1 pound candied pineapple, diced (about 3 cups)
- 1/3 cup best-quality dark rum
- 1 pound butter (room temperature)
- 2 cups sugar
- 7 large eggs
- 1 tablespoon maraschino cherry juice (from bottled maraschino cherries)
- 3 1/2 cups sifted flour (15 3/4 ounces)
- 10 ounces salted macadamia nuts (left whole)
- 1 teaspoon baking powder
- 1/2 teaspoon cream of tartar

Place diced pineapple in a small bowl and cover with the rum. (Best if this is done the night before.) Cream butter and sugar until fluffy, then beat in eggs and cherry juice. Drain pineapple and add the rum to the butter-sugar-egg mixture. Mix 2 cups of the flour with the macadamia nuts and diced pineapple. Sift remaining flour with baking powder and cream of tartar and add to butter-sugar-egg mixture; do not beat, just stir until combined. Now add the pineapple-macadamia-flour mixture and stir again until combined. Spoon into a greased and floured bundt pan (or into smaller ones) and bake in a preheated 325° oven for 30 minutes. Reduce heat to 300° and bake another 45 minutes or longer, or until cake or cakes test done. Cool briefly, then invert on racks to finish cooling.

To prepare ahead of time: Wrap in plastic wrap, then in foil. These will keep at room temperature for 1 week, or for 1 month if refrigerated. They can be frozen for 6 months to 1 year. Always serve at room temperature.

Sponge Cake with Fresh Strawberry Icing

(*serves 12 to 20*)

8 eggs (room temperature)
1 1/2 cups sugar
grated rind of 1 lemon
3 tablespoons lemon juice
1/4 teaspoon salt
1 teaspoon vanilla
1 cup potato starch, measured, then sifted

for fresh strawberry icing

    1/4 cup soft butter (1/2 stick)
    1 pound powdered sugar
    1/2 cup sliced, fresh strawberries

Making the sponge cake: Separate the eggs. Beat egg yolks for 1 minute, then gradually beat in 1 cup of the sugar, grated lemon rind, lemon juice, salt, and vanilla. Beat until mixture is light and fluffy. Lightly fold in sifted potato starch. Beat whites separately until barely stiff, then gradually beat in remaining 1/2 cup sugar. Fold this into egg yolk mixture. Spoon into a large, ungreased angelfood cake pan and bake in a preheated 325° oven for 50 to 60 minutes, or until top springs back when touched with fingers. Invert pan and cool completely, then remove cake from pan.

Making the strawberry icing: Combine ingredients in a food processor and whirl until smooth. (Add more strawberries, or powdered sugar, depending on consistency desired.)

To assemble: Cover cake with strawberry icing. Place on a decorative serving dish and, if desired, surround with large, fresh strawberries.

To prepare ahead of time: This cake can be baked 2 or 3 days ahead; wrap well in foil and leave at room temperature. I think it is best to frost the cake the day you plan to serve it. The cake freezes very well, but preferably without the icing. Defrost, then ice as directed.

Strawberry-Macaroon Cake

(serves 16 to 20)

2 10-inch layers *genoise* (page 185)
chocolate icing (page 187)
3 dozen *almond macaroons* (page 189)
1/2 cup dry sherry
1 1/2 cups strawberry jam
1 1/2 cups heavy whipping cream
chopped pistachios or chocolate sprinkles

To assemble: Cut each cake layer in half, horizontally, thus making 4. Place 1 layer on a cake plate and cover with a layer of strawberry jam. Dip 1 dozen macaroons in sherry and place them on the jam. Sprinkle with a little more sherry. Whip the cream, then cover macaroons with 1/3 of the cream. Place second cake layer on top of this and repeat process. Place third layer on top and again repeat same process. Top with last layer of cake and sprinkle with a little sherry. Cover top and sides with chocolate icing and decorate with chopped pistachios or chocolate sprinkles.

To prepare ahead of time: This can be assembled 1 day ahead; keep well covered and refrigerated. The genoise, macaroons, and chocolate icing can be frozen as directed in those recipes.

Genoise

(*makes 3 9-inch or 2 10-inch layers*)

5 tablespoons butter, melted and cooled
1 1/2 cups sifted cake flour
1/4 teaspoon salt
1 1/2 teaspoons baking powder
6 large eggs (room temperature)
1 1/2 cups sugar
1 teaspoon vanilla

Melt butter and let it cool. Sift flour, salt, and baking powder together and leave it in the sifter. Beat eggs until light, then gradually beat in the sugar and vanilla, beating until fluffy, almost the consistency of whipped cream. Sift flour mixture in gradually, folding it in gently. Fold in cooled butter with a few quick strokes. Pour into layer-cake pans with removable bottoms; lacking those, grease pans, line with waxed paper and grease again. Bake 9-inch layers in a preheated 350° oven for 15 to 20 minutes; if using 10-inch pans, bake at 325° for 30 to 35 minutes. Remove from oven and cool for a few minutes, then invert and remove cakes from pans. Finish cooling cakes on a rack.

To prepare ahead of time: These can be baked 1 or 2 days ahead; wrap carefully in foil and leave at room temperature. Genoise freezes very well. Freeze the layers quickly, then wrap in double foil. (Freezing the cakes before wrapping prevents squashing.)

Chocolate Genoise

(makes 2 9-inch round layers or 1 deep 10-inch cake)

6 large eggs (room temperature)
1 cup sugar
1/4 teaspoon salt
1 teaspoon vanilla
1/2 cup sifted flour (scant 2 1/4 ounces)
1/2 cup unsweetened cocoa
1/2 cup melted butter (1 stick), cooled to room temperature

Place unshelled eggs in a large bowl of hot water to warm them, then break into a mixing bowl and beat until frothy. Gradually beat in sugar, salt, and vanilla (best done with an electric mixer); beat until mixture is the consistency of whipped cream. Sift flour and cocoa together several times, then gradually fold into whipped egg mixture. Fold in melted and cooled butter with a few strokes; don't overmix or the sponge created will be broken down. Pour into greased and lightly floured pans. (For a 10-inch cake, use a springform pan.) Bake in a preheated 350° oven for 15 to 20 minutes; reduce heat to 300° and bake about 10 minutes more (a 10-inch cake will take longer), or until tops spring back when gently touched. Place on racks and let stand for 5 minutes, then remove cakes from pans and finish cooling on cake racks.

To prepare ahead of time: Cakes can be baked 1 day ahead; wrap in foil and leave overnight at room temperature.

To freeze: Wrap well in foil (or freeze quickly first, then wrap in foil).

Chocolate Icing or Filling (Ganache)

(*makes about 2 cups*)

    12 ounces dark sweet chocolate
    1 cup heavy whipping cream

Melt chocolate over hot water. Heat cream, then add it and whisk until smooth. Remove from heat and cool, stirring occasionally, until desired consistency is achieved.

To prepare ahead of time: This can be made a week ahead; keep covered and refrigerated. To use, heat slightly, stirring, until softened to consistency you want.

To freeze: This can be frozen; defrost, then reheat slightly, stirring until softened.

Chocolate Rochettes

    3/4 cup powdered sugar
    1/4 cup cocoa (Dutch if possible)
    4 egg whites
    1/8 teaspoon cream of tartar
    1/8 teaspoon salt
    1/2 cup sugar
    2 1/2 cups slivered almonds, toasted

Sift powdered sugar and cocoa together and set aside. Beat egg whites with cream of tartar and salt until they begin to be stiff, then gradually beat in granulated sugar, beating until very stiff. Fold in cocoa–powdered sugar and then fold in almonds. Place small spoonfuls of this mixture on cookie tins lined with nonstick parchment. Bake in a preheated 300° oven for 10 minutes; reduce heat to 250° and bake until dry and crisp—30 to 45 minutes longer.

To prepare ahead of time: These can be baked 3 weeks ahead; store in airtight tins between layers of waxed paper. Frozen and stored the same way they should keep well for several months.

Tiny chocolate délices

(*makes about 32*)

    4 ounces unsweetened chocolate, melted and cooled to room temperature
    1/4 pound soft butter (1 stick)
    1/2 cup sugar
    3 eggs, separated
    2 tablespoons flour
    1/4 teaspoon salt
    3 egg whites
    2 tablespoons sugar
    chocolate icing (page 187)
    chopped pistachio nuts

Cream butter and 1/2 cup sugar together until light, then add melted chocolate. Add egg yolks, flour, and salt and beat again. In a separate bowl, beat egg whites until barely stiff, then beat in the 2 tablespoons sugar; fold into chocolate mixture. Spoon into about 32 (1 3/4-inch) greased and floured muffin tins. Bake in a preheated 350° oven for 12 minutes. Remove from oven, cool on racks, then remove cakes from tins and ice with chocolate icing; decorate tops with chopped pistachio nuts.

To prepare ahead of time: These can be baked and iced 2 days ahead; keep packed in airtight tins and refrigerated, but bring to room temperature before serving. Frozen, they should keep at least a month.

Almond Macaroons

(*makes 2 to 3 dozen*)

8 ounces canned almond paste
1 cup sugar
3 egg whites

Cut almond paste into cubes, then beat with the sugar until crumbly. Gradually add egg whites and beat slowly until smooth. Place mixture in a pastry bag with a no. 6 round tube and drop on baking pans that have been greased and floured (or on nonstick parchment). Make the macaroons about 3/4-inch in diameter. (If you do not have a pastry bag, drop mixture by teaspoonfuls.) Bake in a preheated 325° oven for 20 to 30 minutes; remove from oven and loosen with a spatula.

To prepare ahead of time: These can be baked 1 week in advance; keep them in airtight tins between layers of waxed paper. The macaroons freeze beautifully.

Chocolate Filbert Spice Cookies

(*makes 3 to 4 dozen*)

1/4 pound filberts, toasted, then skins rubbed off
1/4 pound soft butter (1 stick)
3/4 cup sugar
2 eggs
1/4 pound dark sweet chocolate, melted
2 cups sifted flour (9 ounces)
2 teaspoons baking powder
1/4 teaspoon salt
1 teaspoon cinnamon
1/4 teaspoon *each* of nutmeg, cloves, and mace

Grind filberts in a food processor. Cream butter and sugar, then beat in eggs. Add melted chocolate and ground filberts and stir well. Combine flour, baking powder, salt, and spices, and either sift together several times or mix thoroughly. Add to creamed mixture and stir only enough to combine. Chill for 30 minutes or longer. Divide dough in half and form each portion into a roll 1 to 1 1/2 inches wide. Place on a lightly greased cookie tin and bake in a preheated 350° oven for 25 minutes. Remove from oven, cool briefly, then cut rolls crosswise into slices 1/2 to 3/4 inch thick. Place slices cut sides down on a baking tin and return to oven. Bake 20 to 30 minutes, gradually reducing heat to 225°. Cool, then store in airtight tins between layers of waxed paper.

To prepare ahead of time: These can be baked 1 week ahead and stored at room temperature if packed as directed. They will keep frozen for many months.

Coconut Lace Cookies

(makes 3 to 4 dozen)

1/4 pound butter (1 stick)
3/4 cup sugar
2 tablespoons dark corn syrup
1/4 cup heavy whipping cream
1 2/3 cups flaked canned coconut
1/4 cup sifted flour

Melt butter in saucepan; then add remaining ingredients, stir until well combined, and remove from heat. Drop batter by small teaspoonfuls, at least 4 or 5 inches apart, on cookie sheets lined with nonstick parchment. Bake in a preheated 400° oven for 7 to 9 minutes, or until golden brown. Remove and cool briefly; then, using a spatula, lift cookies onto waxed paper. Store in airtight tins between layers of waxed paper.

To prepare ahead of time: These will keep at room temperature for 10 days, but they must be stored in airtight tins. They will keep for months frozen in airtight containers.

Apricot Bars

(makes about 48 small bars)

for pastry base

> 1 cup unsifted flour (5 ounces)
> 1/4 cup powdered sugar
> 1/4 teaspoon salt
> 1/4 pound butter (1 stick), sliced
> 1 egg, beaten slightly with 1 teaspoon cold water

for filling

> 1 1/4 cups dried apricots (5 ounces)
> zest of 1 lemon
> 1 1/4 cups sugar
> 2 eggs
> 1/4 cup lemon juice
> 1/8 teaspoon salt

Soak apricots in hot water. Make the pastry base while they are soaking.

Making the pastry base: Place flour, powdered sugar, and salt in a food processor and process for 2 seconds. Add sliced butter and process, turning on and off only until butter is distributed and cut into small bits. Add egg-water mixture and process 2 seconds, then remove pastry and form into a flat disk. Chill briefly, then roll out and fit into a 9-inch square pan. Bake in a preheated 350° oven for 20 minutes. Remove and set aside.

Making the filling: Drain apricots, then place them in the food processor; add lemon zest and sugar and process until apricots are finely chopped. Add eggs, lemon juice, and salt, then process, turning on and off, until well mixed, but not puréed. Spoon on top of the prebaked crust and bake in a preheated 350° oven for 30 minutes, or until well browned. Cool, then cut into small squares.

To prepare ahead of time: These can be baked 1 week ahead; store in airtight tins between layers of waxed paper. Frozen and stored the same way they will keep for several months.

Tuiles

(makes 4 or 5 dozen)

4 egg whites
1/4 teaspoon salt
1 cup sugar
1/2 cup melted butter (1 stick)
3 cups sliced, blanched almonds, lightly toasted
1/2 cup sifted flour (2 1/4 ounces)
2 teaspoons vanilla

Beat egg whites with salt and sugar just until barely thickened. Add melted butter and beat again. Combine almonds and flour, then add and stir. Add vanilla. Grease cookie sheets, then dust with flour; or use nonstick parchment. Drop batter by the rounded teaspoonful 3 to 4 inches apart; cookies will spread. Bake in a preheated 350° oven until well browned—about 10 minutes. Remove, and either transfer each to a rolling pin to curl cookies (so that they resemble roof tiles) or leave them flat.

To prepare ahead of time: Packed between layers of waxed paper in airtight tins, these cookies will keep well at room temperature at least 1 week; they will keep for months if frozen.

CRISP SUGAR COOKIES

3/4 pound butter (3 sticks), room temperature
3 cups sugar
2 eggs
grated rind of 1 lemon
2 teaspoons vanilla
6 cups sifted flour (27 ounces)
1 teaspoon baking powder
3/4 teaspoon salt
3/4 cup milk

Cream butter and sugar together until light and fluffy. Beat in eggs, lemon rind, and vanilla. Sift dry ingredients together 3 times, then add them alternately with the milk. Do not beat; just stir until well blended. Chill for several hours or overnight. Divide into 12 portions. Roll 1 portion at a time as thin as possible, meanwhile keeping other portions in the refrigerator. Using cookie cutters, cut into desired shapes and place on greased cookie tins. Bake in a preheated 300° oven for 10 to 15 minutes, or until delicately browned. Remove and cool on waxed paper.

To prepare ahead of time: These can be baked 1 month ahead if stored in airtight tins between layers of waxed paper. Frozen and stored the same way they will keep for months.

Mandelbrodt

(makes about 8 dozen)

    1/4 pound butter (1 stick), room temperature
    2 1/2 cups sugar
    3 teaspoons vanilla
    6 eggs
    6 1/4 cups sifted flour (28 1/4 ounces)
    1 1/2 teaspoons salt
    3 teaspoons baking powder
    2 cups chopped almonds, lightly toasted

Cream butter and sugar, then beat in vanilla and eggs. Combine flour, salt, and baking powder, then gradually stir into creamed mixture. Stir in toasted almonds. Chill for 30 minutes or longer. Divide dough into 4 parts, and form each into a long roll about 1 1/2 inches wide. Place on lightly greased baking pans and bake in a preheated 350° oven for 25 to 30 minutes. Remove from oven and cool for 5 minutes, then slice rolls into 1 1/2-inch slices. Place slices cut sides down on baking pans and return to a 350° oven until lightly toasted and dry; watch that they do not burn, reducing oven heat if necessary. This toasting process may take 30 minutes or longer.

To prepare ahead of time: These will keep at room temperature for 2 weeks if packed between layers of waxed paper in airtight tins. Frozen and packed the same way, they will keep for months.

Mandelschnitten

(makes about 4 dozen small bars)

for pastry

    1 2/3 cups sifted flour (7 1/4 ounces)
    2 tablespoons sugar
    1/4 teaspoon salt
    1/4 teaspoon baking powder
    1/4 pound cold butter (1 stick)
    1 extra-large egg
    1/4 cup heavy whipping cream

for filling

    1 1/2 cups sugar
    1/2 cup honey
    1/2 cup heavy whipping cream
    1/4 pound butter (1 stick)
    2 cups slivered almonds

Making the pastry: Combine flour, sugar, salt, and baking powder and place in a food processor. Cut butter in slices, add to flour mixture, and process briefly by turning machine on and off—until butter is the size of small peas. Beat egg and cream together, then add to flour-butter mixture and process only until mixture begins to form around blade; do NOT overprocess. Remove, form into a ball or flat disc, wrap and chill at least 1 hour (or overnight).

Baking the pastry: Roll pastry into a rectangle about 12 by 18 inches and gently lift into a jelly-roll pan (10 1/2 by 15 1/2 inches). Pat into the pan, covering bottom and sides. Prick pastry with a fork, then chill for 20 minutes or longer. Bake in a preheated 375° oven for 12 minutes, until it begins to turn golden. Remove from oven and set aside.

Making the filling: Combine sugar, honey, cream, and butter in a heavy saucepan and bring to a boil, stirring constantly. Reduce heat to moderate and add slivered almonds. Cook, stirring occasionally, until mixture reaches 240° on a candy thermometer, or until a drop forms a soft ball in cold water. Remove from heat, cool half a minute, then pour into prebaked shell.

Baking the mandelschnitten: Bake filled shell in a preheated 375° oven for 15 minutes; reduce heat to 350° and bake another 8 to 10 minutes, or until filling has turned a caramel color. Cool briefly on a rack, then divide in 4 parts, and with the aid of a large spatula, lift each out onto greased foil. Cool completely, then cut into bars about 1 by 2 inches.

To prepare ahead of time: These will keep well in airtight containers between layers of waxed paper at room temperature for 1 week; frozen they will keep for months.

Apple Pie with Cinnamon Ice Cream

(*serves about 8*)

6 large green apples (need 7 cups sliced apples)
1 1/4 cups sugar
3 tablespoons flour
1/4 teaspoon salt
1/4 teaspoon nutmeg
1 teaspoon cinnamon
2 teaspoons lemon juice
rich pastry (page 210)
cinnamon ice cream (page 243)

Core, peel, and thinly slice apples. In a separate bowl mix sugar, flour, salt, nutmeg, and cinnamon together. Roll out half the pastry and line a 10-inch pie pan. Combine sliced apples and sugar mixture and toss well, then spoon into pastry-lined pan. Sprinkle with lemon juice. Roll out other half of pastry and cover apples. Press 2 crusts together firmly, using cold water to seal them. Prick top crust, or cut a design, and then bake in a preheated 425° oven for 50 to 60 minutes—until juices begin to bubble. If pastry browns too quickly, reduce oven heat somewhat. Serve hot or warm topped with a generous scoop of cinnamon ice cream.

To prepare ahead of time: The pie can be baked 1 day before; keep refrigerated. To serve, cover lightly with foil and reheat in a 350° oven. The pie freezes well; defrost, then cover with foil and reheat in a 350° oven.

Paradisaical Hot Apple Tarts

(*serves 4*)

    3/4 to 1 pound *puff pastry* (page 211)
    4 large cooking apples (pippins are especially good)
    12 tablespoons melted butter (1 1/2 sticks)
    8 tablespoons sugar
    whipped cream

Roll out pastry very thin (about 1/16 inch thick). Cut into 8-inch circles (use an 8-inch plate as guide). Place circles on baking pans (with sides) and chill thoroughly or freeze. Peel, quarter, and slice apples (as thin as possible), and arrange slices on the pastry circles, overlapping them to form a flower design. Sprinkle with HALF the butter and with HALF the sugar and bake in a preheated 425° oven for 20 minutes. Remove from oven and sprinkle with remaining butter and sugar; then return to oven for another 10 to 15 minutes. Serve hot on warm plates, with whipped cream offered separately.

To prepare ahead of time: The puff pastry circles can be frozen, but they should be wrapped carefully in foil if you plan to store them for several months; use them directly from the freezer. The tarts can be partially baked in the morning (the first 20 minutes); when almost ready to serve, add remaining butter and sugar and finish baking as directed.

Apple Dumplings with Apricot Sauce

(*makes 6 to 8*)

rich pastry (page 210)
6 medium-size green apples (or 8 small ones)
1 cup sugar
1/4 teaspoon nutmeg
1 teaspoon cinnamon
2 to 3 tablespoons butter
1 egg, beaten slightly

for apricot sauce

    1/2 pound dried apricots
    1/2 cup sugar
    1/2 teaspoon almond extract

Making the apricot sauce: Wash apricots, place in a saucepan, cover with water, and soak several hours; then bring to a boil and simmer until soft. Purée with the sugar and almond extract. Taste, and add more sugar if desired.

Making the apple dumplings: Peel and core apples. Combine sugar, nutmeg, and cinnamon. Roll out pastry and cut into squares large enough to completely envelop apples. Place 1 apple on each square and brush pastry around apple with the egg. Divide sugar mixture over the apples, dot with butter, then bring up pastry corners and seal at the top. Brush with egg and bake in a preheated 425° oven for 10 minutes; reduce heat to 375° and bake 50 to 60 minutes longer. Serve warm with apricot sauce.

To prepare ahead of time: These can be baked 1 day ahead and refrigerated, or they can be frozen. In either case, bring to room temperature, then reheat in a 350° oven. The apricot sauce can be made 3 days ahead; it can also be frozen.

French Lemon Tart, My Way

(*serves about 8*)

> *rich pastry* (page 210) or *sweet pastry* (page 210), enough for a 10-inch shell
> 4 eggs
> 1 cup sugar
> grated rind of 3 lemons
> 2/3 cup lemon juice
> 1/8 teaspoon salt
> 3 tablespoons soft butter

Roll out pastry and fit into a 10-inch loose-bottomed tart pan. Line with greased foil and weight with dried beans, then bake in a preheated 400° oven for 10 minutes. Remove beans and foil, reduce heat to 350°, and bake an additional 10 to 15 minutes. Cool, then remove shell from tin and place it on a cookie sheet.

Making the filling: Combine eggs, sugar, grated lemon rind, lemon juice, and salt in an enamel or stainless steel saucepan. Whisk over moderate heat until thickened. Remove from heat, add butter, and cool, stirring occasionally, until lukewarm.

To assemble and bake: Spoon filling into prebaked shell and bake in the lower part of a preheated 350° oven for 10 minutes; move to upper part of oven, increase heat to 425°, and bake another 5 to 10 minutes. Cool on rack, then serve at room temperature.

To prepare ahead of time: The pastry shell can be baked 1 day ahead, or it can be baked and frozen. The lemon filling can be made 1 day ahead; cover and refrigerate. Assemble and bake the day you plan to serve.

Fresh peach tart

(*serves about 6*)

rich pastry (page 210) or *sweet pastry* (page 210),
   1/2 recipe of either
3 large fresh peaches, peeled and sliced (3 1/2 cups)
1 tablespoon lemon juice
3 tablespoons melted butter
1/2 cup brown sugar (pack to measure)
1/4 cup granulated sugar
1/8 teaspoon salt

Roll pastry into a large circle, then fit into a 10-inch flan pan (with loose bottom). Chill thoroughly. Combine peaches with lemon juice and melted butter, then add both kinds of sugar and salt and stir gently. Spoon into chilled shell and bake in a preheated 450° oven (on lowest shelf) for 15 minutes; reduce heat to 400° and bake an additional 15 minutes. Remove from oven and cool briefly. Serve warm.

To prepare ahead of time: This can be baked 1 day before; cover and refrigerate. To serve, reheat in a 350° oven. This can be frozen too; defrost, then reheat in a 350° oven.

Blue Plum Tart

(*serves 4 to 6*)

rich pastry (page 210), 1/2 recipe
1 tablespoon sugar
1/2 cup graham cracker crumbs
1 pound blue plums, pitted and halved
1/3 cup sugar
3 tablespoons powdered sugar
1/4 teaspoon cinnamon

Line an 8-inch pie pan (preferably with a loose bottom) with pastry. Sprinkle pastry with the 1 tablespoon sugar and the graham cracker crumbs. Arrange halved plums on top and sprinkle with the 1/3 cup sugar. Bake in a preheated 450° oven for 20 minutes, then reduce heat to 350° and bake another 20 to 30 minutes or until plums are well glazed and juices have begun to bubble. (If pastry gets too dark, cover top of tart loosely with foil.) Remove from oven and cool on a rack for 15 minutes. Sift powdered sugar and cinnamon together, then sprinkle over plums. Serve at room temperature.

To prepare ahead of time: This can be baked 1 day ahead and refrigerated, or it can be baked and frozen. Underbake slightly if doing this ahead, then bring to room temperature, finish baking, and sprinkle with sugar-cinnamon mixture.

Phyllo Cheese Pastries in a Rumanian Mode

(*makes about 20*)

2 pounds phyllo
1 1/2 to 2 pounds melted butter

for cheese filling

    1 1/2 pounds dry farmers cheese
    8 ounces cream cheese
    1/2 cup melted butter (1 stick)
    1 cup plus 2 tablespoons sugar
    1 teaspoon salt (or to taste)
    4 eggs
    2 teaspoons vanilla
    grated rind of 2 lemons

Making the cheese filling: Put farmers cheese through a food mill or whirl in a food processor. Place in a large mixing bowl and gradually add remaining ingredients, beating them together until smooth and light. Chill for several hours or overnight.

Making the pastries: For each pastry you will need 2 sheets of phyllo. (Cover remaining phyllo, first with waxed paper and then with a damp towel, to prevent drying and crumbling.) Place 1 on a flat surface and brush with melted butter. Place second sheet on top and brush again with butter. Fold sheets lengthwise to form a long, narrow rectangle. Place a heaping tablespoon of cheese filling in the lower right corner of the rectangle and fold over to form a triangle. Turn left side of long rectangle over to prevent cheese from oozing out, then brush with melted butter and continue to fold over, keeping the triangular shape—as one folds a flag—and brushing with butter as you fold. Place pastries on lightly greased pans (with sides) and bake in a preheated 425° oven for 10 minutes. Reduce heat to 325° and bake another 15 to 20 minutes. Serve hot with a generous sprinkling of powdered sugar.

To prepare ahead of time: These can be baked 1 day ahead, wrapped, and refrigerated, but underbake slightly. They can be frozen too, but again, underbake slightly. Bring to room temperature, then finish baking just before serving.

Congress tarts

(*makes about 24*)

rich pastry (page 210)
raspberry jam

for filling

>1/4 pound butter (1 stick)
>1/2 cup plus 2 tablespoons sugar
>2 eggs
>1 1/4 cups blanched almonds, ground
>1 1/2 teaspoons almond extract

Making the filling: Cream butter and sugar until light and fluffy. Beat in eggs, then stir in ground almonds and almond extract.

Making the tarts: Roll out pastry to 1/8-inch thickness and cut circles about 3 inches in diameter. Line shallow patty-shell pans with pastry circles. Place 1/2 teaspoon raspberry jam in the bottom of each and then cover each with a small spoonful of the filling. Decorate tops with two strips of pastry (use leftover after rolling circles) arranged like a cross. Bake in a preheated 425° oven for approximately 15 minutes. Remove from oven and carefully remove tarts from pans; cool them on racks.

To prepare ahead of time: These tarts can be baked 3 days ahead, wrapped tightly, and refrigerated. They can be baked and frozen, and will keep for months. In either case, bring to room temperature and freshen them in a 350° oven.

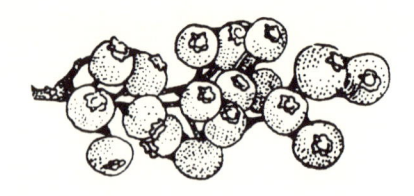

CARAMEL-WALNUT TART WITH CHOCOLATE GLAZE

(*serves 16 to 20*)

for pastry

    3 1/8 cups sifted flour (14 ounces)
    1/3 cup sugar
    1/2 pound butter (2 sticks) plus 2 tablespoons
    1 egg
    6 to 8 tablespoons cold water

for caramel-walnut filling

    1 1/2 cups sugar
    1/2 cup water
    1/3 cup honey
    3/4 cup butter (1 1/2 sticks)
    3 1/2 cups coarsely chopped walnuts, lightly toasted
    scant 1 cup milk

for chocolate glaze

    6 ounces semi-sweet chocolate
    1/4 cup butter (1/2 stick)
    toasted walnut halves (optional)

Making the pastry: Mix flour and sugar together, then cut in the butter until mixture resembles soft crumbs. (Can do this either with a pastry blender or in a food processor.) Place in a large bowl. Beat egg with 6 tablespoons water and add to flour mixture. Cut in with a knife, then combine, using your hands, to form a mass; add up to 2 more tablespoons of water if necessary. Wrap in foil and chill 30 minutes or longer.

Making the filling: Combine sugar, water, and honey in a heavy saucepan and bring to a boil over moderate heat. Wash down crystals on side of pan with a wet paper towel wrapped around a fork. Boil over medium heat until mixture turns a medium caramel color. Remove from heat and add butter. Stir until melted, then add walnuts and milk. Return to heat, bring to a boil, then reduce heat and simmer for 20 minutes, stirring occasionally. While this is cooking, proceed with rolling out the pastry.

To assemble and bake: Lightly grease a sideless baking tin and place a loose-bottomed 11-inch tart pan on it. Grease inside of tart pan—sides and bottom. Roll out 2/3 of pastry into a 14-inch circle and fit into tart pan, leaving about a 1/2-inch overhang. Chill while walnut filling is cooking. Remove walnut filling from heat and cool about 2 minutes, then fill shell. Roll out remaining 1/3 of pastry to a 12-inch circle and place over filling. Wet pastry edges with water and seal top to bottom pastry. Trim as needed. Bake in a preheated 425° oven for 20 minutes. Turn off oven and leave tart in oven for an additional 15 minutes. Remove tart to rack and cool about 3 hours. Invert tart onto a large serving plate and cover with glaze, decorating if desired with toasted walnut halves. Chill briefly for easier serving.

Making the chocolate glaze: Melt chocolate over hot water, then beat in the butter. Use as directed above.

To prepare ahead of time: This tart will keep up to ten days, covered and refrigerated.

To freeze: The pastry freezes beautifully; and the entire tart can be frozen with or without the chocolate glaze.

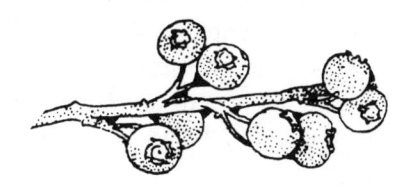

Raspberries on Puff Pastry with Caramel Sauce

(*serves 8*)

4 cups fresh raspberries
1 pound *puff pastry* (page 211)
2 cups *pastry cream* (page 248)
1 cup heavy whipping cream
2 tablespoons kirsch

for caramel sauce

    1 cup sugar
    1/3 cup boiling water
    1 cup heavy whipping cream

Making the caramel sauce: Melt sugar in a skillet over moderate heat, stirring often. Turn heat to lowest possible point, then add boiling water. Be careful—it may sputter. Stir over low heat until water and sugar have completely combined. Add cream, return to heat, and bring to a boil. Simmer 1 minute and remove from heat. Chill or leave at room temperature.

Making the filling: Whip the 1 cup of cream, then fold into pastry cream and add kirsch. Cover and chill.

Baking the pastries: Roll puff pastry to a 1/4-inch thickness, then cut into rectangles about 3 by 4 inches and place them on a baking sheet. Chill at least 30 minutes. Score tops lightly with a fork, and if desired brush tops with a little beaten egg. Chill again for at least 15 minutes, then bake in a preheated 425° oven for 10 minutes. Reduce heat to 375° and bake another 10 minutes, or until well browned. Remove from oven, cut each in half horizontally, remove any soft, uncooked pastry, and set aside at room temperature.

To serve: Reheat pastries in a 275° oven only long enough to freshen them. Place pastry bottoms on individual plates, top with some filling and with raspberries and cover with pastry tops. Surround with more raspberries and serve caramel sauce separately.

To prepare ahead of time: Pastry filling can be prepared 1 day before; keep covered and refrigerated. Caramel sauce can be prepared 1 week before if kept covered and refrigerated. (Puff pastries can be cut in shapes and kept frozen if desired; bake directly from freezer.) Pastries can be baked the morning of the day you plan to serve; leave them loosely covered at room temperature, then proceed as directed in recipe.

Rich Pastry

(enough for a 9-inch 2-crust pie)

2 1/4 cups sifted flour (10 1/4 ounces)
1/2 teaspoon salt
6 ounces butter (1 1/2 sticks)
1 egg
4 tablespoons cold water

Mix flour and salt together, then cut in the butter. Combine egg and water and beat slightly. Pour over flour-butter mixture and cut in with a knife until all dry ingredients are absorbed. Turn out on a lightly floured board and knead gently—2 or 3 times. Chill at least 1 hour before using.

To prepare ahead of time: This can be prepared several days ahead; keep well wrapped in the refrigerator. This pastry freezes well too.

Sweet Pastry

(enough for 2 9-inch pie shells)

2 cups sifted flour (9 ounces)
1/4 teaspoon salt
1/3 cup sugar
6 ounces cold butter, sliced (1 1/2 sticks)
2 extra-large eggs

Combine flour, salt, and sugar in a food processor. Add butter and process until butter is size of small peas. Beat eggs lightly with a fork, then add and process briefly, ONLY UNTIL PASTRY BEGINS TO COLLECT ON THE BLADE. Remove, then knead once or twice. Wrap and chill at least 1 hour, or overnight.

To prepare ahead of time: This can be made several days ahead; keep well wrapped in the refrigerator. It freezes well too.

Puff Pastry

(*makes 3 1/2 pounds*)

for butter paste

>1 1/4 pounds butter (5 sticks)
>4 ounces cake flour (about 1 1/4 cups sifted)

for flour paste

>1 pound all-purpose flour (about 4 cups sifted)
>1 teaspoon salt
>1 1/2 cups ice water

Making the butter paste: Mix butter and cake flour together in a bowl with a wooden spoon, or with an electric dough hook. Chill for 10 minutes.

Making the flour paste: Mix all-purpose flour and salt together, then add ice water and stir until combined. Do NOT beat or overmix. Chill for 10 minutes.

To roll and fold pastry: (see illustration on page 212)

Step 1: Roll out flour paste to a rectangle 12 by 18 inches and mark in thirds. Divide butter paste in half and place half in the center 1/3 of rolled-out flour paste. Fold 1/3 over butter paste, then arrange remaining butter paste on top and cover with remaining 1/3 of flour paste. Pat down, wrap in waxed paper, and chill 30 minutes.

Step 2: Arrange folded pastry so that open edges face you. Roll out into a rectangle 18 by 30 inches. Fold ends to middle, then fold double (like a book) and press gently but firmly. Turn pastry again so that edges face you, and roll again into a rectangle 18 by 30 inches, and again fold ends to middle and then fold double. Press firmly, wrap again in waxed paper, and chill for 30 minutes.

Step 3: Repeat the 2 rollings described in Step 2, but now wrap carefully in plastic wrap and chill at least several hours—better overnight. [*continued on next page*]

Note: Please observe that the pastry is first rolled and folded in thirds, chilled for 30 minutes; next it is twice rolled and folded in fourths, then chilled; and finally it is again twice rolled and folded in fourths, then wrapped for a final chilling of at least several hours or overnight.

To prepare ahead of time: Puff pastry can be prepared 2 to 3 days ahead; keep well wrapped and refrigerated. It freezes extremely well; freeze in portions you think you will need, or roll into shapes desired and freeze those. In all cases the pastry should be double-wrapped for freezer storage.

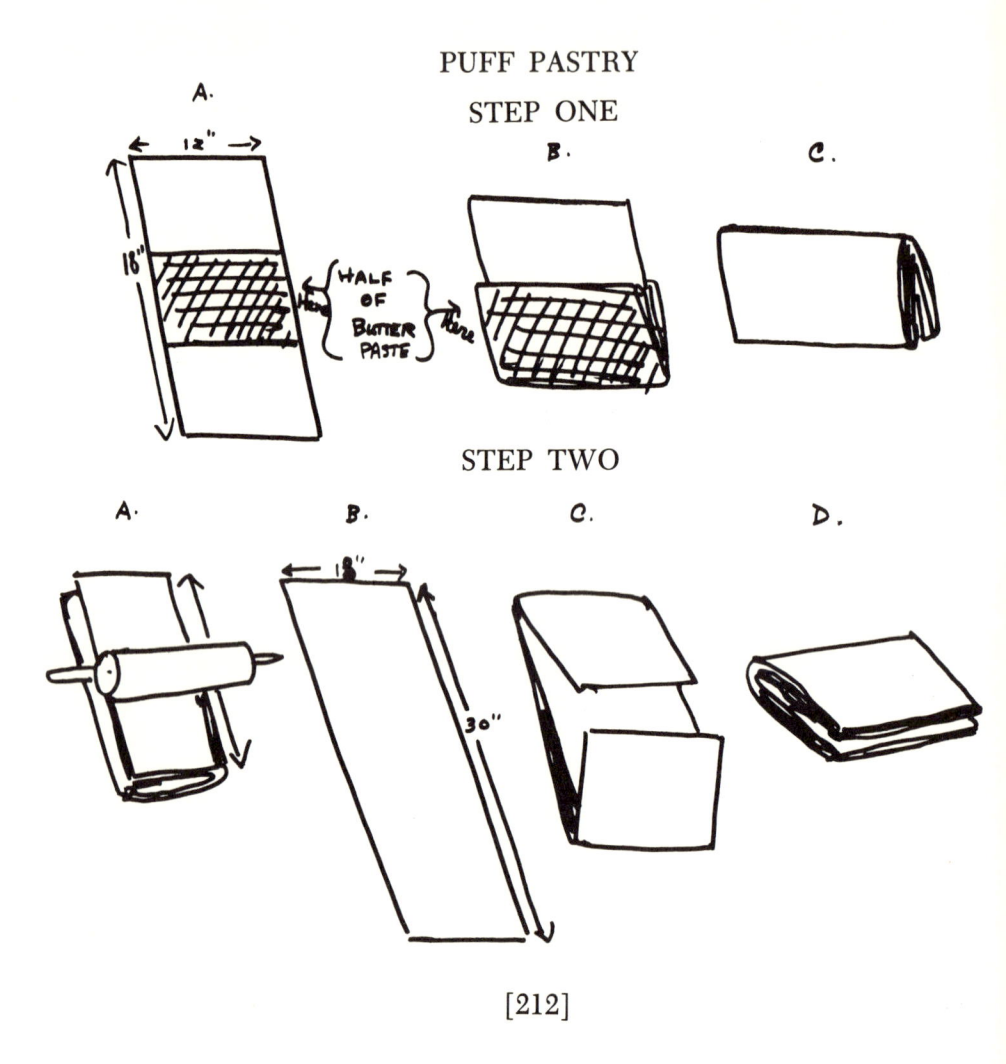

PUFF PASTRY

STEP ONE

STEP TWO

Desserts

MERINGUES WITH FRESH ORANGES AND CARAMEL-ORANGE SAUCE

(*serves 6 to 8*)

6 to 8 individual *meringue shells* (page 247)
1 quart *vanilla ice cream* (page 241)
fresh orange segments

for caramel-orange sauce

    1 orange
    2 cups sugar
    1 cup water

Making the caramel-orange sauce: Peel orange with a potato peeler, thus removing only the orange part and none of the white pith. Cut peel into tiny strips. Melt sugar in a heavy skillet over moderate heat and cook, stirring occasionally, until sugar has caramelized. Remove from heat and wait 1 minute, then carefully add water. When bubbling has stopped, return to moderate heat and stir until a thin syrup has formed. Add orange peel strips and cook 1 minute. Remove from heat and cool.

To serve: Place meringues on dessert plates, then scoop ice cream into meringues. Arrange orange segments around meringues and spoon caramel-orange sauce over ice cream.

To prepare ahead of time: Meringue shells can be baked 2 weeks ahead or frozen. Caramel-orange sauce can be made 1 week ahead and kept refrigerated; *but* serve at room temperature. Orange segments can be prepared 1 day ahead and refrigerated. And if your freezer has the space, you can fill your dessert dishes with the meringues and scooped ice cream in the morning.

Meringues with Chocolate Sauce and Walnut Praline

(*serves 6 to 8*)

6 to 8 individual *meringue shells* (page 247)
1 quart *vanilla ice cream* (page 241)

for chocolate sauce

>2 ounces unsweetened chocolate
>1 tablespoon butter
>1/3 cup boiling water
>1 cup sugar
>2 tablespoons light corn syrup
>1 tablespoon butter
>1 teaspoon vanilla
>grated rind of 1 orange

for walnut praline

>1 cup sugar
>1 cup walnuts

Making the chocolate sauce: Melt chocolate and 1 tablespoon butter over low heat and stir. Add boiling water and stir until blended, then add sugar and corn syrup. Stir over very low heat until mixture begins to boil, then cook over moderate heat without stirring for 4 or 5 minutes. Remove from heat and cool for 1 minute, then stir in butter and vanilla. Add grated orange rind and set aside.

Making the walnut praline: Melt sugar in a skillet, stirring over moderate heat until sugar caramelizes. Add walnuts and stir. As soon as well combined, pour into a greased metal pan. Cool completely, then chop, pound, or grind to make the praline. Keep in a tightly sealed glass jar in a cool place.

To serve: Place meringues on dessert plates, then scoop vanilla ice cream into meringues. Pour reheated chocolate sauce over ice cream and top with a generous sprinkling of walnut praline.

To prepare ahead of time: Meringue shells can be baked 2 weeks ahead or frozen. Chocolate sauce can be made 1 week ahead and kept refrigerated. Praline can be made weeks ahead and kept refrigerated, or frozen for months. And if your freezer has the space, your dessert dishes can be filled with the meringues and scooped ice cream in the morning, ready to finish just before serving.

Apple Shortcakes with Lemon Sauce

(*serves 6*)

3 large, green apples (5 cups sliced)
2 tablespoons butter
3/4 cup sugar
2 tablespoons lemon juice
soft butter

for shortcake

> 2 cups sifted flour (9 ounces)
> 4 teaspoons baking powder
> 1/2 teaspoon salt
> 1/4 pound butter (1 stick)
> 1 egg
> 1/3 cup milk

for lemon sauce

> 1/2 cup sugar
> 1 tablespoon cornstarch
> 1/8 teaspoon salt
> 1 cup cold water
> grated rind of 1 lemon
> 2 to 4 tablespoons lemon juice (to taste)
> 1 tablespoon butter

Making apple filling: Peel and slice apples. Melt the 2 tablespoons butter in a large skillet, add apples, 3/4 cup sugar, and 2 tablespoons lemon juice. Cover and cook over moderate heat, stirring occasionally, until apples are barely tender (but not mushy). Remove from heat and place in bowl. Cover and leave at room temperature.

Making the shortcakes: Place flour, baking powder, and salt in food processor. Slice butter and add, then process until butter is distributed and the size of tiny peas. Remove to a large bowl. Beat egg with milk, then add to mixture and cut in with a knife until mixture forms a mass. (Add more milk only if needed.) Place on a lightly floured board and knead a few times, then pat or roll out to a 1/2-inch thickness. Cut in 3-inch rounds and place on greased (or nonstick) baking tins and refrigerate until needed.

Making the lemon sauce: Combine sugar, cornstarch, and salt in a saucepan and stir well. Add cold water and stir until smooth. Add grated lemon rind and cook over moderate heat, stirring constantly, until mixture boils. Reduce heat and simmer for 2 minutes. Remove from heat and stir in lemon juice and butter. Set aside; reheat later.

Baking the shortcakes: Place shortcakes in a preheated 450° oven and bake for 10 minutes. Reduce heat to 400° and bake another 5 minutes or until well browned and crisp.

To assemble and serve: Split individual shortcakes and generously butter lower half of each; place on dessert plates. Top with a generous spoonful of cooked apples and cover with the upper half of the shortcakes. Serve at once with hot lemon sauce.

To prepare ahead of time: The apples and lemon sauce can be prepared 2 days ahead; cover and refrigerate. Bring apples to room temperature and reheat lemon sauce before serving. The shortcakes can be rolled out and refrigerated in the morning; bake just before serving.

CHOCOLATE AND WHIPPED CREAM DREAM

(serves 12 to 16)

for chocolate cake

    4 ounces semi-sweet chocolate
    1/4 pound butter (1 stick)
    1/2 cup sugar
    4 eggs
    1/2 teaspoon vanilla

for whipped cream layer

    2 cups heavy whipping cream
    2 tablespoons sugar
    1 teaspoon vanilla
    1 teaspoon unflavored gelatin
    2 tablespoons cold water

for chocolate topping

    9 ounces semi-sweet chocolate
    2/3 cup strong coffee
    2 teaspoons butter

seedless raspberry jam

Making the cake: Melt chocolate and cool slightly. Cream butter and sugar, then beat in eggs, and stir in chocolate and vanilla. Pour into a greased jelly-roll pan (10 1/2 by 15 1/2 inches) and bake in a preheated 325° oven for 25 to 30 minutes. Leave in pan and cool on a rack.

Making the whipped cream layer: Whip the cream, gradually beating in sugar and vanilla, but only until barely stiff. Soak gelatin in cold water for 5 minutes, then dissolve it to a syrup by placing it over simmering water. Add it all at once to whipped cream, beating cream at the same time; beat only until stiff.

Making the chocolate topping: Melt chocolate with the coffee, remove from heat and stir in butter. Cool slightly. (Reheat later if necessary.)

To assemble: Cover cake (leaving it in the baking pan) with a thin layer of raspberry jam, and then spread whipped cream evenly on the cake. Chill for 1 hour. Pour chocolate topping (make sure it is liquid but not hot) on top of whipped cream, tilting pan to spread it; do not use a knife. One good way to do this: pour it on in criss-cross lines, then tilt pan to fill in. Chill thoroughly, then cut in squares to serve.

To prepare ahead of time: Chocolate cake can be baked 2 days ahead; cover with foil and keep refrigerated. The entire dessert can be completed in the morning; keep chilled until time to serve.

Crustless Cheesecake

(*serves 8 to 12*)

2 (8-ounce) packages cream cheese
1 cup sugar
7 extra-large eggs
1 1/2 teaspoons vanilla
grated rind of 1 lemon
2 tablespoons lemon juice
2 tablespoons flour
1/4 teaspoon salt
1/2 teaspoon cream of tartar

to serve with

>sweetened strawberries
>*or* raspberries
>*or* hot *chocolate sauce* (page 216 or page 236)

Whip cream cheese with 3/4 cup of the sugar. Separate eggs, then beat yolks into cheese mixture, and also the vanilla, lemon rind, lemon juice, and flour. In another bowl, beat whites with salt and cream of tartar until barely stiff, then gradually beat in remaining 1/4 cup sugar. Fold mixtures together and pour into a well-greased Pyrex casserole (7 1/2 by 12 by 2 inches) and place in a larger pan. Add boiling water to larger pan and bake in a preheated 325° oven for 1 hour. Turn oven heat off, but leave cake in oven for an additional 15 minutes. Remove cake from oven and larger pan and cool on a rack. Serve at room temperature accompanied with sweetened strawberries or raspberries or hot chocolate sauce.

To prepare ahead of time: This can be prepared 1 day ahead; keep covered and refrigerated, but bring to room temperature before serving. It can be frozen too, but the texture will not be quite as delicate.

CHOCOLATE-ORANGE POTS DE CRÈME

(*serves about 8*)

2 cups heavy whipping cream
1/4 cup sugar
8 ounces dark sweet chocolate
6 egg yolks
grated rind of 1 orange
1 tablespoon Grand Marnier

Heat cream and sugar together in a saucepan over low heat until sugar has dissolved. Add chocolate and stir constantly until mixture is smooth. Beat egg yolks in a bowl, then gradually pour hot mixture over them, beating all the while. Return to lowest heat (or to the top of a double boiler) and whisk or stir constantly until mixture is thick. Remove from heat and stir in grated orange rind and Grand Marnier. Spoon into pots de crème or into demitasse cups. Chill thoroughly.

To prepare ahead of time: These can be prepared up to 2 days ahead. Keep covered and refrigerated.

CHOCOLATE CHEESECAKE

(serves about 20)

for crumb crust

>1 1/2 cups graham cracker crumbs
>1/4 cup sugar
>6 tablespoons melted butter

for cheesecake

>40 ounces (5 8-ounce packages) cream cheese
>2 cups sugar
>1/4 cup flour
>3 egg yolks
>5 whole eggs
>1/4 teaspoon salt
>1 cup sour cream
>12 ounces dark sweet chocolate, melted
>3 tablespoons dark rum

for whipped cream garnish

>2 cups heavy whipping cream
>1/4 cup sugar (or to taste)
>1/4 cup cognac

Making the cheesecake: Combine ingredients for crumb crust in a bowl and then press mixture on sides and bottom of a 10-inch springform pan. Chill at least 15 minutes. Beat cream cheese at medium speed until smooth, then gradually beat in the sugar. Add flour and remaining ingredients, beating only until smooth and blended. Pour into prepared pan and bake in a preheated 475° oven for 10 minutes. Reduce heat to 300° and bake an additional 50 minutes. Turn off oven heat, but leave cheesecake in oven for another 30 minutes. Cool on a cake rack, then remove sides of springform pan, wrap and refrigerate until about 1 hour before serving.

Making whipped cream garnish: Whip cream until almost stiff, then beat in sugar and cognac. Decorate top of cheesecake with this, or serve separately and let guests help themselves.

To prepare ahead of time: This can be prepared and refrigerated 2 to 3 days before serving.

To freeze: This can be frozen for several months. Defrost slowly in the refrigerator; it will take 36 to 48 hours. It is best to remove it from the refrigerator an hour or more before serving unless the whipped cream garnish has been added.

CRÊPES WITH WALNUTS AND CHOCOLATE SAUCE IN THE HUNGARIAN STYLE

(*serves 12*)

84 tiny (2 1/2-inch) *crêpes* (page 27)
chocolate sauce (either page 216 or page 236)
melted butter

for walnut filling

    4 cups walnuts, toasted, then finely chopped
    1 cup sugar
    grated rind of 2 oranges
    1 cup golden raisins, soaked in hot water, then drained
    1 cup fine-quality medium-dark rum
    1/4 cup melted butter (1/2 stick)
    1/2 cup milk

If possible, prepare crêpes in that wonderful Swedish pan with the 7 shallow indentations; lacking that skillet, cook them as small as you can in a large nonstick skillet.

Making the walnut filling: Combine walnuts, sugar, and orange rind and stir. Soak raisins in the rum, then add to walnuts with melted butter and milk. Stir until well combined. Set aside at room temperature.

To assemble: Stack 7 crêpes with walnut filling in between each—either in individual shallow casseroles or arranged in stacks in larger shallow casseroles. Do not put walnut filling on the top crêpe. Spoon melted butter on each, cover with foil and set aside until time to heat.

To serve: Place foil-covered casseroles in a preheated 350° oven for 15 to 20 minutes, or until very hot. Serve with chocolate sauce—best if it is hot, but let guests help themselves.

To prepare ahead of time: Crêpes can be made in advance as directed in that recipe. Chocolate sauce can be made several days (or a week) ahead; keep refrigerated and reheat before serving. Walnut filling can be made 3 days ahead; keep covered and refrigerated but bring to room temperature 4 hours before filling crêpes.

Frozen Grand Marnier Bonbons

Grand Marnier ice cream (page 244)

for dipping bonbons

    12 ounces semi-sweet chocolate
    4 tablespoons vegetable oil (*not* olive oil)

Making the bonbons: Using a melon scoop, scoop tiny balls from Grand Marnier ice cream and freeze them until solid on small foil pans.

Making the dipping mixture: Melt chocolate and oil together in the top of a double boiler over barely simmering water, stirring constantly. Remove and let stand until room temperature.

To dip: Dip scooped ice cream balls in the chocolate, removing only 6 to 8 of them from the freezer at a time—keep the rest frozen until the first batch is finished. Place dipped bon bons on waxed paper in foil pans and return immediately to freezer; then begin another batch. After all have been dipped and completely frozen, stack them in airtight tins between layers of waxed paper and keep frozen.

To serve: Serve Grand Marnier bonbons on chilled plates, directly from freezer.

To prepare ahead of time: These should keep well for several weeks if stored in a freezer that maintains an even cold temperature.

CASSATA ALLA SICILIANA

(*serves 16 to 24*)

2 (10-inch) layers of *genoise* (page 185)

for ricotta filling

> 1/2 cup finely chopped candied orange peel
> 2/3 cup finely chopped candied cherries
> 1/4 cup shelled and blanched pistachio nuts
> 1/2 cup rum
> 2 tablespoons Grand Marnier
> 3 pounds ricotta cheese
> 1 cup sugar
> 1 cup semi-sweet chocolate chips

for whipped cream frosting

> 1 1/2 teaspoons unflavored gelatin
> 2 tablespoons cold water
> 3 cups heavy whipping cream
> 1/2 cup sugar
> 1 tablespoon Grand Marnier

for decoration

> 1/2 cup candied cherries, quartered
> 1 cup toasted almonds

Preparing the ricotta filling: Combine orange peel, cherries, and pistachio nuts with the rum and the 2 tablespoons of Grand Marnier; let soak for 1 hour. Whip ricotta with the 1 cup sugar until light and fluffy, then drain fruit-nuts mixture, reserving the remaining rum and Grand Marnier. Beat in fruit and nuts, and stir in chocolate chips.

Preparing the whipped cream frosting: Soak gelatin in the 2 tablespoons cold water for 5 minutes, then dissolve over hot water. Whip cream until almost stiff, gradually adding the 1/2 cup sugar and 1 tablespoon of Grand Marnier. Add dissolved gelatin all at once, beating at same time, but only until cream is stiff. Do not overbeat.

To assemble: Cut each layer of genoise in half horizontally, making 4 layers. Place 1 layer on a large dessert platter; sprinkle with about 2 tablespoons of the reserved rum and Grand Marnier, and cover with 1/3 of the ricotta filling. Repeat with 2 more layers, then top with the fourth layer and sprinkle with remaining liqueurs. Frost top and sides with the whipped cream frosting and decorate with quartered cherries and toasted almonds. Chill until time to serve.

To prepare ahead of time: The entire dessert can be made the day before serving; keep covered and refrigerated. The genoise layers can be frozen as directed in that recipe.

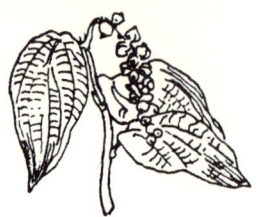

Individual Dacquoise with Coffee Filling

(serves 12 to 20)

for filbert meringue circles

    8 egg whites
    1 cup sugar
    1 cup filberts, toasted, skins rubbed off, then ground
    1 tablespoon plus 1 teaspoon cornstarch
    3 tablespoons sugar

for coffee buttercream filling

    8 egg yolks
    1 cup less 2 tablespoons sugar (6 ounces)
    1 1/2 cups heavy whipping cream
    1 1/3 cups sugar (10 ounces)
    1/4 cup instant powdered coffee
    1 pound unsalted butter, sliced

for decoration

    more toasted filberts, crushed or coarsely chopped
    powdered sugar

Making the filbert meringue circles: Combine egg whites and the 1 cup sugar in a mixing bowl. Place over simmering water and stir constantly until mixture is barely warm. Remove from heat and whip until stiff. Combine ground filberts with cornstarch and the 3 tablespoons of sugar; fold into beaten whites. Cover baking tins with nonstick parchment, and mark parchment with 40 2-inch circles or 24 3-inch circles. Pipe out meringue (or use a small spatula) on the circles. Bake in a preheated 275° oven for about 1 hour or until firm, lightly browned, and crisp. Remove from oven, cool on racks, then remove meringues from parchment.

Making the coffee buttercream filling: Beat egg yolks with the 6 ounces of sugar until light and fluffy. Bring the cream and the 10 ounces of sugar to a boil, stirring occasionally. Stir in the powdered coffee, then pour this into yolk mixture, beating all the while. Return to a large saucepan and cook over moderate heat, stirring, until cream has thickened. Remove to a mixing bowl and whip at moderate speed until mixture reaches room temperature. Add butter in slices, a few at a time, whipping at moderate speed. After butter has been incorporated, chill mixture until it is of spreading consistency.

To assemble: Cover half the meringue circles with a generous layer (about 3/4 inch thick) of coffee filling; top with remaining meringues. Cover the outside edges of each with crushed filberts and sprinkle tops with powdered sugar. Refrigerate until time to serve.

To prepare ahead of time: Coffee buttercream filling can be prepared several days ahead; keep refrigerated, but bring to spreading consistency at room temperature before filling meringues. Meringues can be baked 10 days ahead; store between layers of waxed paper in airtight tins. Meringues and coffee filling can be frozen, but freeze them separately. Defrost, then fill as directed.

CARAMEL LACE BASKETS WITH PRALINE ICE CREAM AND FRESH FRUIT

(*serves 10*)

1 1/2 quarts *praline ice cream* (page 245)
thin slices *genoise* (page 185), or substitute split commercial ladyfingers
kirsch
10 large strawberries
50 fresh bing cherries
10 tiny bunches seedless grapes

for caramel lace baskets

>3/4 cup butter (1 1/2 sticks)
>1/2 cup brown sugar (pack to measure)
>1/4 cup sugar
>1/2 cup dark corn syrup
>2 teaspoons vanilla
>1 1/2 cups sifted flour (6 3/4 ounces)

Making the caramel lace baskets: Melt butter in a saucepan, then stir in brown and white sugars and corn syrup. Stir over low heat until sugar has dissolved. Remove from heat and beat in vanilla and flour. Cool to room temperature. Bake 2 at a time by dropping batter from a large spoon onto a lightly greased cookie sheet. They will spread greatly during the baking. Bake in a preheated 300° oven for 10 to 12 minutes, or until golden brown. Remove from oven and let stand briefly, then lift wafers with the aid of a spatula and place them over bowls, molding them into basket shapes. Remove when cool—they will then be hard and crisp. Repeat process with remaining batter. Store in airtight tins between layers of waxed paper.

To assemble and serve: Place a small piece of genoise, or half a ladyfinger, in bottom of each lace basket. Sprinkle lightly with a little kirsch. Fill each with a small scoop of praline ice cream and top with a strawberry. Surround each lace basket with 5 cherries and a bunch of grapes.

To prepare ahead of time: The caramel lace baskets will keep for several weeks if packed in airtight tins between layers of waxed paper; they can be frozen for 3 to 4 months.

Raspberries on Genoise with Whipped Cream

(*serves 8 to 12*)

    1 (9-inch) layer of *genoise* (page 185)
    3 baskets of fresh raspberries
    1/2 cup sugar (or to taste)
    1/3 cup kirsch
    1/2 cup water
    1 tablespoon cornstarch
    1 cup heavy whipping cream, whipped and sweetened to taste

Cover genoise with about 2/3 of the raspberries. Combine remaining raspberries (there should be about 1 cup) with the sugar, kirsch, water, and cornstarch, and stir thoroughly. Slowly bring to a boil, stirring constantly; then cook over moderate heat until mixture has thickened. Remove from heat, cool, and spoon over the raspberries on the genoise cake. Decorate with the sweetened whipped cream; chill for 1 hour or longer, then serve cold.

To prepare ahead of time: Genoise freezes, as directed in that recipe. The cake can be covered with raspberries and glazed in the morning; keep chilled. Add whipped cream shortly before serving.

Raspberries or Strawberries on Leaves

> fresh raspberries—pick over but do not wash
>   OR
> fresh strawberries—wash quickly, drain, and dry
>   on paper towels
> granulated sugar in a large sugar shaker
> *crème fraîche* (page 28)
>   OR
> heavy whipping cream, whipped
> lemon leaves, or any kind of leaves that are non-toxic

This is mostly a beautiful arrangement, but somehow it magnifies the lovely taste of berries and cream. If possible use the charming wooden baskets in which berries sometimes are stored in the market. (I have saved these baskets over the years, washed them in soap and water and dried them thoroughly.) Line baskets, or failing those, large dessert bowls, with leaves, then arrange berries on the leaves. Serve them with a dessert plate, fork, and spoon and let your guests have the pleasure of arranging them on their plates and seasoning them with sugar and cream to their tastes.

To prepare ahead of time: Raspberries or strawberries can be arranged in the morning; leave at room temperature. Crème fraîche can be made up to 10 days ahead. If using whipping cream, it can be whipped in the morning; refrigerate and stir gently before serving.

GRAND MARNIER FROZEN SOUFFLÉS

(*serves 6 to 8*)

4 egg yolks
3/4 cup sugar
1/2 cup water
2 cups heavy whipping cream
10 to 12 tablespoons Grand Marnier
4 ladyfingers, lightly toasted in oven

for decoration

fresh raspberries or candied orange-peel strips

Beat egg yolks with an electric beater until very light. Combine sugar and water in a saucepan and stir over moderate heat until sugar has dissolved, then boil for 2 minutes without stirring. Gradually add this hot syrup to the egg yolks, and beat it slowly but constantly until very thick; then beat in 2 tablespoons of Grand Marnier. In another bowl, whip cream until thick, gradually beating in 2 tablespoons Grand Marnier, then fold into yolk mixture. Soak ladyfingers in 6 to 8 tablespoons of Grand Marnier. Prepare individual soufflé dishes with waxed paper collars that rise 1 inch above the top of dishes (tie collars on with string). Fill each dish halfway with soufflé mixture. Add half a soaked ladyfinger, then fill each to the top of the collars with remaining soufflé mixture. Freeze, remove collars, then decorate with fresh raspberries or candied orange-peel strips.

To prepare ahead of time: These can be made 1 day ahead and left in the freezer uncovered. They can be made several weeks ahead of time, but in that case they should be wrapped carefully after they are frozen.

Vanilla Ice Cream with Brandied Cherries and Chocolate Sauce

(*serves 8*)

1 quart *vanilla ice cream* (page 241)
brandied bing cherries (page 249)

for chocolate sauce

>8 ounces dark sweet chocolate
>1 cup heavy whipping cream
>rum or cognac to taste

Making the chocolate sauce: Combine chocolate and cream and stir over low heat until well blended; add rum or cognac. Serve hot or at room temperature.

To assemble and serve: Scoop vanilla ice cream into individual dessert dishes; then press down in the center of each, making a small well. Fill centers with 6 brandied bing cherries and about 1 tablespoon of the juice. Bring to table and pass chocolate sauce separately.

To prepare ahead of time: The cherries must be prepared at least 1 week ahead (as the recipe indicates, they can be made up to 1 year ahead). The chocolate sauce can be made 1 week ahead; keep refrigerated. Bring to room temperature before serving, or reheat if you want to serve it hot. If your freezer is large enough, scoop ice cream into dessert dishes in the morning and store them there until time to serve.

Grapefruit Sorbet

(makes about 1 quart)

2 1/2 cups fresh grapefruit juice
1/2 cup sugar (or to taste)
1 scant teaspoon unflavored gelatin

Soak gelatin in 3 tablespoons grapefruit juice for 5 minutes. Heat this over simmering water until gelatin forms a syrup, then add to remaining grapefruit juice and stir immediately and thoroughly. Add sugar, and stir until sugar has dissolved. Chill, then freeze in an ice cream machine.

To prepare ahead of time: This will keep well in a freezer for 1 month or longer, but it must be stored in an airtight container in a freezer that maintains an even cold temperature.

Lemon Sorbet

(makes about 1 1/2 quarts)

2 1/2 cups water
1 3/4 cups sugar
1 1/2 teaspoons unflavored gelatin
1/2 cup cold water
grated rind of 2 lemons
1 cup lemon juice

Combine the 2 1/2 cups water and sugar and cook over moderate heat, stirring until sugar has dissolved. Soak gelatin in cold water for 5 minutes, then add to hot mixture and stir until dissolved. Remove from heat and add lemon rind and lemon juice. Cover and chill thoroughly, then freeze in an ice cream machine.

To prepare ahead of time: This will keep well in a freezer for 2 months or longer, but it must be stored in airtight containers in a freezer that maintains an even cold temperature.

Orange Sorbet

(makes about 1 quart)

1 1/4 teaspoons unflavored gelatin
1/4 cup cold water
1 cup sugar
3/4 cup water
grated rind of 1 orange
2 cups fresh orange juice
2 tablespoons lemon juice

Soak gelatin in the 1/4 cup cold water. Combine sugar and 3/4 cup water in a saucepan and stir over moderate heat until sugar has dissolved; then stir in soaked gelatin and remove from heat. Add orange rind, orange juice, and lemon juice; stir, then chill thoroughly. Freeze in an ice cream machine.

To prepare ahead of time: This should keep well for 1 month or longer in a tightly sealed container in a freezer that maintains an even cold temperature.

Peach Sorbet

(makes about 1 quart)

2 1/2 cups fresh peach purée
2 tablespoons lemon juice
1 1/4 cups sugar (or to taste)
1 or 2 tablespoons Amaretto or Maraschino liqueur
red or yellow food coloring

Combine purée, lemon juice, sugar, and liqueur, and stir until sugar has dissolved. Add either a few drops of red (to tint pink), or a few each of red and yellow (to tint a light peach color). Chill thoroughly, then freeze in an ice cream machine.

To prepare ahead of time: This should keep for 1 month or longer in a tightly sealed container in a freezer that maintains an even cold temperature.

Pear Sorbet

(makes about 1 quart)

4 medium to large ripe pears, peeled, diced, and puréed (need 2 cups purée)
1 teaspoon unflavored gelatin
1/4 cup cold water
1 cup sugar
3/4 cup water
1/4 cup lemon juice
3 tablespoons pear eau-de-vie

Soak gelatin in the 1/4 cup cold water for 5 minutes. Combine sugar and 3/4 cup water and cook over low heat, stirring, until sugar has dissolved. Stir in soaked gelatin, and as soon as it has dissolved, remove from heat. Add pear purée, lemon juice and the eau-de-vie. Chill thoroughly, then freeze in ice cream machine.

To prepare ahead of time: This will keep well in the freezer for 2 months or so, but it must be stored in an airtight container in a freezer that maintains an even cold temperature.

Raspberry Sorbet

(makes about 1 quart)

1 1/4 teaspoons unflavored gelatin
1/4 cup cold water
1/2 cup sugar
1/3 cup water
2 (10-ounce) packages frozen raspberries, puréed and strained— discarding seeds
3 tablespoons Framboise liqueur

Soak gelatin in the 1/4 cup cold water for 5 minutes. Combine sugar and 1/3 cup water and stir over moderate heat until sugar has dissolved, then stir in soaked gelatin. Add to strained raspberries and mix well. Add Framboise and chill thoroughly. Freeze in an ice cream machine.

To prepare ahead of time: This should keep well for 1 month or longer in a tightly sealed container in a freezer that maintains an even cold temperature.

Strawberry Sorbet

(makes about 1 quart)

2 (10-ounce) packages frozen strawberries, defrosted
1 1/2 teaspoons unflavored gelatin
1/4 cup cold water
1/2 cup sugar
1/3 cup water
3 tablespoons strawberry liqueur or kirsch

Whirl strawberries in a food processor and place in a bowl. Soak gelatin in the 1/4 cup cold water for 5 minutes. Combine the sugar and 1/3 cup water in a saucepan and heat, stirring, until sugar has dissolved, then stir in soaked gelatin. Add to strawberries and stir well; then add liqueur. Chill thoroughly; then freeze in an ice cream machine.

To prepare ahead of time: This should keep well for 1 month or longer in a tightly sealed container in a freezer that maintains an even cold temperature.

Watermelon Sorbet

(makes about 1 1/2 quarts)

1 1/2 teaspoons unflavored gelatin
1/4 cup lemon juice
4 cups puréed fresh watermelon (need about 6 cups cubed)
1 cup sugar (or to taste)
1/4 cup kirsch

Soak gelatin in lemon juice for 5 minutes. Dissolve gelatin by placing it over hot water and stirring until it becomes a syrup. Stir into puréed watermelon and add sugar and kirsch. Stir occasionally until sugar has dissolved, then chill thoroughly. Freeze in an ice cream machine.

To prepare ahead of time: This will keep several weeks or longer in a tightly sealed container in a freezer that maintains an even cold temperature.

Frozen Orange Delicious

(makes about 1 quart)

1/4 cup lemon juice
1 1/2 cups fresh orange juice
grated rind of 2 oranges
1/2 cup light corn syrup
2/3 cup sugar
1 1/3 cups milk

Combine all ingredients and stir until sugar has dissolved, then chill thoroughly. Freeze in an ice cream machine.

To prepare ahead of time: This should keep at least 1 month in a tightly sealed container in a freezer that maintains an even cold temperature.

Vanilla Ice Cream

(makes about 1 quart)

3/4 cup sugar (scant)
1/8 teaspoon salt
1 cup milk
4 egg yolks
2 cups heavy whipping cream
3 to 4 teaspoons vanilla

Dissolve sugar and salt in the milk over moderate heat. Beat egg yolks and then pour hot milk mixture over yolks, beating all the while. Return to saucepan and stir constantly over lowest heat until custard coats spoon. Remove from heat and stir in whipping cream and vanilla. Chill thoroughly, then freeze in an ice cream machine.

To prepare ahead of time: This should keep well for 1 month or longer in a tightly sealed container in a freezer that maintains an even cold temperature.

Rich dark chocolate ice cream

(makes about 1 quart)

3/4 cup sugar (scant)
6 ounces semi-sweet chocolate
1 cup milk
4 egg yolks
1/8 teaspoon salt
2 teaspoons vanilla
2 cups heavy whipping cream

Dissolve sugar and chocolate in the milk over low heat, stirring constantly until mixture is very hot and smooth. Beat egg yolks with salt, then pour chocolate mixture over the yolks and beat well. Add vanilla and cream and stir well, then chill thoroughly. Freeze in an ice cream machine and store in an airtight container in the freezer.

To prepare ahead of time: This should keep well for 1 month or longer in a tightly sealed container in a freezer that maintains an even cold temperature.

Coffee ice cream for coffee lovers

(makes about 1 1/2 quarts)

1 1/4 cups sugar
5 level tablespoons instant coffee
1 cup milk
pinch of salt
3 cups heavy whipping cream

Dissolve sugar, salt, and coffee in the milk in a saucepan over moderate heat. Add heavy whipping cream, stir, then chill thoroughly; freeze in an ice cream machine.

To prepare ahead of time: This should keep 1 month or longer in a tightly sealed container in a freezer that maintains an even cold temperature.

Cinnamon Ice Cream

(*makes about 1 quart*)

1/2 cup sugar
4 teaspoons cinnamon
3 tablespoons water
1 cup milk
1/2 cup sugar
1/8 teaspoon salt
1 egg
2 cups heavy whipping cream
1 teaspoon vanilla

Combine 1/2 cup sugar and cinnamon in a saucepan and stir well. Add the 3 tablespoons water and slowly bring to a boil, stirring constantly. Simmer for 2 minutes, then remove from heat and cool to room temperature. Place milk and the 1/2 cup sugar and salt in a saucepan and stir over moderate heat until sugar has dissolved. Beat egg and pour hot milk mixture over egg, stirring, then return to saucepan and stir over lowest heat until a thin custard has formed. Remove from heat and combine with the cream, cinnamon syrup, and vanilla. Chill thoroughly, stir again, then freeze in an ice cream machine.

To prepare ahead of time: This should keep 1 month or longer in a tightly sealed container in a freezer that maintains an even cold temperature.

Grand Marnier Ice Cream

(makes about 1 quart)

2/3 cup sugar (scant)
1/8 teaspoon salt
1 cup milk
4 egg yolks
2 cups heavy whipping cream
grated rind of 1 orange
2 tablespoons Grand Marnier

Dissolve sugar and salt in the milk over moderate heat. Beat egg yolks and then pour hot milk mixture over yolks, beating all the while. Return to saucepan and stir constantly over lowest heat until custard coats spoon. Remove from heat and stir in whipping cream, grated orange rind, and Grand Marnier. Chill thoroughly, then freeze in an ice cream machine.

To prepare ahead of time: This should keep well for 1 month or longer in a tightly sealed container in a freezer that maintains an even cold temperature.

Peach Ice Cream

(makes about 1 1/2 quarts)

2 cups mashed fresh peaches
1 tablespoon lemon juice
1 1/4 cups sugar (or to taste)
1 cup milk
2 cups heavy whipping cream
1/8 teaspoon salt
red or yellow food coloring

Combine mashed peaches with lemon juice. Dissolve sugar in the milk, then add to peaches. Add cream and salt and stir well. Add either a few drops of red (to tint pink), or a few of yellow (to tint pale yellow), or a few of each color (to tint a light peach color). Chill thoroughly, then freeze in an ice cream machine.

To prepare ahead of time: This should keep well for 1 month in a tightly sealed container in a freezer that maintains an even cold temperature.

Praline Ice Cream

(makes about 1 quart)

    1/2 cup sugar (scant)
    1/8 teaspoon salt
    1 cup milk
    4 egg yolks
    2 cups heavy whipping cream
    1 teaspoon vanilla
    1 cup *praline paste* (page 248)

Dissolve sugar and salt in the milk over moderate heat. Beat egg yolks and then pour hot milk mixture over yolks, beating all the while. Return to saucepan and stir constantly over lowest heat until custard coats spoon. Remove from heat and stir in whipping cream and vanilla. Chill thoroughly, then freeze in an ice cream machine. Remove from machine and stir in the 1 cup of praline paste, then store in the freezer in tightly sealed containers.

To prepare ahead of time: This should keep well for 1 month or longer in tightly sealed containers in a freezer that maintains an even cold temperature.

Fresh Strawberry Ice Cream

(makes about 1 quart)

    2 1/2 cups fresh mashed strawberries
    3/4 to 1 cup sugar (to taste)
    2 cups heavy whipping cream
    pinch of salt

Combine all ingredients and stir until sugar has dissolved. Chill thoroughly; then freeze in an ice cream machine.

To prepare ahead of time: This should keep well for 1 month or longer in a tightly sealed container in a freezer that maintains an even cold temperature.

Fresh Pineapple and Rum Ice Cream

(makes about 1 1/2 quarts)

2 cups finely chopped fresh pineapple
1 1/2 cups sugar (or to taste)
1/4 cup light rum
2 tablespoons dark Jamaican rum
2 cups heavy whipping cream

Combine all ingredients and stir occasionally until sugar has dissolved. Chill thoroughly, then freeze in an ice cream machine.

To prepare ahead of time: This will keep for 1 month or longer in a tightly sealed container in a freezer that maintains an even cold temperature.

Ginger Ice Cream

(makes a generous quart)

1/2 cup sugar
1/8 teaspoon salt
1 cup milk
4 egg yolks
2 cups heavy whipping cream
1 cup chopped preserved ginger (6 to 8 ounces)
2 tablespoons ginger syrup (from jar of preserved ginger)

Dissolve sugar and salt in the milk over moderate heat. Beat egg yolks, then pour hot milk mixture over yolks and stir well. Return to heat and cook over lowest temperature until a thin custard forms. Remove from heat; add cream and ginger syrup. Chill thoroughly, then freeze in an ice cream machine. Stir in the chopped ginger and freeze in a tightly sealed container.

To prepare ahead of time: This will keep for 1 month or longer in a tightly sealed container in a freezer that maintains an even cold temperature.

Rum, chestnut, and cherry ice cream

(makes about 1 1/2 quarts)

    1 cup sliced (or small pieces) preserved, candied chestnuts
    1 cup halved candied cherries
    3/4 cup finest golden or dark rum
    1 recipe of *vanilla ice cream* mixture (page 241), made with a scant 1/2 cup sugar and *no* vanilla)

Marinate the chestnuts and cherries in the rum overnight, at room temperature. Next day, prepare vanilla ice cream mixture, adding to it the rum-liquid left from marinating the chestnuts and cherries. Chill thoroughly, then freeze in an ice cream machine. Stir in the chestnuts and cherries, then freeze in a tightly sealed container. *Note*: This will not get as hard as other ice creams because of the amount of alcohol it contains.

To prepare ahead of time: This will keep several weeks or longer in a tightly sealed container in a freezer that maintains an even cold temperature.

Meringue shells

    4 large egg whites (room temperature)
    pinch of salt
    pinch of cream of tartar
    1 1/4 cups sugar
    1/2 teaspoon vanilla (optional)

Beat egg whites with the salt and cream of tartar until barely stiff, then gradually beat in about 2/3 of the sugar and vanilla. Fold in remaining sugar. Bake meringues on waxed-paper-lined baking tins in a preheated 275° oven until dry and crisp (about 1 hour or longer). Remove from oven and cool, then store in containers with tight-fitting lids.

To prepare ahead of time: Meringues can be baked 2 weeks ahead; keep in tightly closed containers at room temperature. They freeze well; store in tightly closed containers. They can be used directly from the freezer.

Pastry Cream Favorite

1/2 cup sugar
1/4 cup flour
1/8 teaspoon salt
1 1/2 cups milk
4 egg yolks
1 teaspoon vanilla

Combine sugar, flour, and salt in a bowl and mix together thoroughly. Add milk and whisk. Place in top of a double boiler and cook, stirring, until very hot. Beat egg yolks in a separate bowl, then pour warm mixture over yolks, beating at the same time. Return to top of double boiler and cook, stirring constantly, until mixture is very thick (about 12 minutes). Remove from heat and cool over ice and water, stirring occasionally. Stir in vanilla. Cover and chill.

To prepare ahead of time: This can be made 1 day before; keep covered and refrigerated.

Praline Paste

2 cups sugar
1 cup blanched almonds
1 cup filberts, toasted, then skins rubbed off

Place sugar in a large heavy skillet. Melt sugar slowly to a caramel over moderate heat, stirring occasionally. Add almonds and filberts and stir over lowest heat until they are completely coated with caramel. Pour at once into a greased metal pan. Place on a rack and let it cool and harden. Chop, pound, or if wanting a paste, break it up and whirl in a food processor (or blender) until it is a powder. Store in tightly sealed jars.

To prepare ahead of time: This will keep for several months in the refrigerator if stored in tightly sealed jars; it will keep at least a year stored in the freezer.

Brandied bing cherries

    3 quarts pitted fresh bing cherries
    4 cups sugar
    1 1/2 cups cognac or fine-quality California brandy

Combine ingredients in a large bowl and stir well. Cover and refrigerate; stir daily for about 1 week or until sugar has dissolved completely. Store cherries and liquid in glass jars with tight-fitting covers and keep refrigerated.

To prepare ahead of time: These will keep a year or possibly longer if kept refrigerated.

Index

Ahead-of-time combination salad, 145
Almonds
  Cassata alla siciliana, 228
  Chicken "country captain" style, 70
  Chocolate rochettes, 187
  Cinnamon-meringue cake, 174
  Filling, 205
  Macaroons, 189
  Mandelbrodt, 195
  Mandelschnitten, 196
  Mexican chicken with green sauce, 68
  Praline paste, 248
  Spinach-romaine salad, 147
  Trout cornmealed, 50
  Tuiles, 193
Alsatian onion pie, 3
Anchovies
  Antipasto, 12
  Green goddess dressing, 150
  And pimento canapés, 14
Anna's smoked haddock mousse, 20
Antipasto, big party, 12
Appetizers and first courses
  Alsatian onion pie, 3
  Anna's smoked haddock mousse, 20
  Antipasto, 12
  Asparagus in puff pastry, 8
  Avocado fontainebleau, 26
  Avocados filled with lobster, 17
  Canapé cakes (two), 18
  Chicken liver mousse, 15
  Chicken liver pâté with port wine aspic, 16
  Chiles en nogada, 24
  Crêpe appetizer gâteau, 23
  Eggs deluxe with caviar, 22
  Herring with apple, onion, and dill, 14
  Mushroom-phyllo hot pastries, 10
  Mushroom tartlets, 11
  Pimento-anchovy canapés, 14
  Rumaki with watermelon pickles, 6
  Salmon and sole pâté, 13
  Shrimp and sole mousse in cabbage, 4
  Tuscan bean and tunafish appetizer, 25

  Wing-drumsticks with sesame seeds, 7
Apples
  Dumplings, with apricot sauce, 200
  With herring, onion, and dill, 14
  Paradisaical hot tarts, 199
  Pie, 198
  And Prune stuffing, 83
  Shortcake, with lemon sauce, 218
Apricots
  Bars, 192
  Dried, in fruited rice, 122
  Sauce, 200
Artichokes
  Bottoms (shrimp and mushrooms in phyllo), 56
  Hearts (green goddess seafood salad), 150
Asparagus
  A Chinese way, 125
  In puff pastry, 8
Aspics
  Port wine, for chicken liver pâté, 16
  Sherry, for smoked haddock mousse, 20
Avocados
  Cobb salad, 143
  Fontainebleau, 26
  Guacamole, 42
  With lobster, 17
  Tomato and honeydew melon salad, 141
Bacon
  Cobb salad, 143
  Romaine and bean sprout salad, 146
  Spaghetti carbonara, 107
  Spinach and orange salad, 148
  Spinach, romaine, and almond salad, 147
Bean sprouts and romaine salad, 146
Beans
  Refried, in beef burritos, 115
  White, and tunafish appetizer, 25
Beef
  Boiled, with horseradish sauce, 92
  Burritos, 115

Short ribs with sauerkraut, 93
Steak in crêpes with madeira sauce, 90
Tenderloins in a spicy sauce, 89
Beets, pickled, and red onion salad, 142
Black forest torte, 176
Blue plum tart, 203
Boiled beef with horseradish sauce, 92
Boned chicken breasts in phyllo, 72
Braised red cabbage, 127
Brandied bing cherries, 249
Breads
  Brioche, 161
  Corn, 170
  Cornmeal yeast, 159
  Rye, French crusty, 158
Burritos, beef, 115
Butter, clarified, 28
Butter rolls, 160

Cabbage
  Red, braised, 127
  Red, and raisin, onion slaw, 141
  Shrimp and sole mousse, in, 4
Cakes
  Almond-cinnamon-meringue, 174
  Black forest torte, 176
  Chocolate genoise chantilly, 175
  Chocolate and whipped cream dream, 220
  Deluxe pound, 181
  Genoise, 185
  Grand finale chocolate gâteau, 178
  Lemon, 173
  Macadamia-pineapple-rum, 182
  Sponge, 183
  Strawberry-macaroon, 184
Cantaloupe
  Chicken salad in, 149
  Red pepper and romaine salad, 142
Caramel
  Lace baskets, 232
  Orange sauce, 215
  Sauce, 208
  Walnut tart with chocolate glaze, 206
Carrots and celery, 128
Cassata alla siciliana, 228
Caviar, eggs deluxe, with, 22
Celery
  And carrots, 128
  Chicken salad in cantaloupe, 149

In combination salad, 145
And white corn, 128
Cheese
  Crêpe appetizer gâteau, 23
  Feta, shrimp Greek style, 58
  Filling, lasagne rolls, 110
  Gougère, 117
  Green corn tamales, 116
  Phyllo pastries, 204
  With potatoes and onions, 136
  Sauce, 126
  Spinach phyllo strudel, 132
  See also Cream cheese; Feta cheese; Parmesan cheese
Cheesecake
  Chocolate, 224
  Crustless, 222
Cherries
  Black forest torte, 176
  Brandied bing, 249
  With vanilla ice cream, 236
  Candied, cassata alla siciliana, 228; and
  Rum and chestnut ice cream, 257
Chestnuts, candied (rum and cherry ice cream), 247
Chicken
  Breasts
    Boned, in phyllo, 72
    In corn chips, 71
    "Country captain" style, 70
    Majestic, 74
    Monte Alban en papillote, 66
    With seedless grapes, 76
  Cobb salad, 143
  Enchiladas, 114
  Fried, old-fashioned, 67
  Mexican with green sauce, 68
  Roasted, pomegranate, 63
  Salad in cantaloupe, 149
  Stan and Don's, in papaya, 69
  Waterzoöi, 64
  Wing-drumsticks with sesame seeds, 7
Chicken livers
  Mousse super simple, 15
  Pâté with port wine aspic, 16
  Rumaki with watermelon pickles, 6
Chiles, green
  En nogada, 24
  Fish fillets, Mexican style, 37

Green corn tamales, 116
Mexican chicken with green sauce, 68
Chocolate
  Cakes
    Black forest torte, 176
    Genoise, 186
    Genoise chantilly, 175
    Grand finale gâteau, 178
    And whipped cream dream, 220
  Chantilly, 175
  Cheesecake, 224
  Crêpes with walnuts and chocolate sauce, 226
  Filbert spice cookies, 190
  Filling
    Black forest torte, 176
    Ganache, 187
    Orange, 178
  Frozen Grand Marnier bonbons, 227
  Glaze, 206
  Icing (Ganache), 187
  Orange pots de crème, 223
  Rich dark ice cream, 242
  Rochettes, 186
  Sauce, 216, 236
  Tiny délices, 188
Cinnamon
  Almond-meringue cake, 174
  Ice cream, 243
  Rolls, family-style, 164
Cobb salad, 143
Coconut lace cookies, 191
Coffee
  Buttercream filling, 230
  Ice cream, 242
Coffeecakes
  Cinnamon rolls, family-style, 164
  Danish pastry pecan rolls, 168
  Honey-walnut rolls, 162
  Walnut, 166
Congress tarts, 205
Cookies
  Apricot bars, 192
  Chocolate filbert spice, 190
  Chocolate rochettes, 187
  Coconut lace, 191
  Mandelbrodt, 195
  Mandelschnitten, 196
  Sugar, 193
  Tuiles, 193

Corn
  Simply baked, 129
  Tamales, green corn, 116
  White, and celery, 128
Cornbread, 170
  Stuffing, 78
Corn chips, chicken breasts in, 71
Cornmeal yeast bread, 159
Court bouillon, 42
Crabmeat
  Enchiladas, 112
  Seafood salad, hot, 59
  Shrimp and oyster gumbo, 60
Cream
  Crème fraîche, 28
  Whipped
    Filling, 220
    Frosting, 228
    Garnish, 224
Cream cheese and walnut sauce, 24
Crêpes, 27
  Appetizer gâteau, 23
  Steak in, with madeira sauce, 90
  With walnuts and chocolate sauce, 226
Crisp sugar cookies, 194
Crisp water rolls, 157
Crustless cheesecake, 222
Cucumbers
  Combination salad, 145
  Greek salad with fennel and feta, 145
Currants with wild rice and pine nuts, 121

Dacquoise with coffee filling, 230
Danish pastry pecan rolls, 168
Deluxe pound cake, 181
Dill, fresh
  Cantaloupe, red pepper, and romaine salad, 142
  Greek salad with fennel and feta, 145
  Green mayonnaise, 154
  With herring, apple, and onion, 14
  Neptune's favorite shrimp, 54
  Sour cream dressing, 153
  Spinach phyllo strudel, 132
Ducklings
  With orange sauce, 82
  With peaches, 81
  With pineapple, 80
Dumplings, apple, 200

Duxelles, 72

Eggs
  Deluxe with caviar, 22
  Hard-boiled
    Anna's smoked haddock mousse, 20
    Cobb salad, 143
    Dressing for boston lettuce, 144
    Green goddess seafood salad, 150
    Russian buffet salad, 151
    Two canapé cakes, 18
  Omelet, smoked turkey, 120
  Scrambled, with spinach roll, 118
  Spaghetti carbonara, 107
  Whites
    Almond-cinnamon-meringue cake, 174
    Almond macaroons, 189
    Chocolate rochettes, 187
    Crisp water rolls, 157
    Halibut mousse, 46
    Meringue shells, 247
    Salmon and sole pâté, 13
    Sole mousse, 4, 36
    Tiny chocolate délices, 188
    Tuiles, 193
  Yolks
    Brioche, 161
    Chicken liver pâté, 16
    Chocolate cheesecake, 224
    Chocolate-orange pots de crème, 223
    Ginger ice cream, 246
    Grand Marnier frozen soufflés, 235
    Grand Marnier ice cream, 244
    Green mayonnaise, 154
    Pastry cream favorite, 248
    Praline ice cream, 245
    Sauce Alma, 34
    Stan and Don's chicken in papaya, 69
    Trout "La Pyramide," 48
    Vanilla ice cream, 241
    Waterzooï chicken, 64
Enchiladas
  Chicken, 114
  Crabmeat, 112

Family-style cinnamon rolls, 164
Fennel
  And green grape salad, 144
  Greek salad with feta, 145
Feta cheese
  Greek salad with fennel, 145
  Shrimp Greek style, 58
  Spinach phyllo strudel, 132
Fettucine Alfredo-Mellinkoff, 109
Filberts
  Chocolate spice cookies, 190
  Meringue circles, 230
  Praline paste, 248
Fish and seafood
  Anchovy-pimento canapés, 14
  Antipasto, 12
  Avocados filled with lobster, 17
  Crabmeat enchiladas, 112
  Crab, shrimp, and oyster gumbo, 60
  Fish fillets, Mexican style 37
  Fish stock, 46, 48
  Green goddess seafood salad, 150
  Haddock mousse, Anna's smoked, 20
  Halibut mousse, 46
  Herring with apple, onion, and dill, 14
  Lobster tails with butter and lemon, 52
  Lobster with waterchestnuts, 51
  Pike baked with vegetables and red wine, 44
  Poached whole fish with guacamole, 42
  Salmon and sole pâté, 13
  Salmon en papillote, 31
  Salmon with champagne sauce, 32
  Salmon steaks in foil packets, 33
  Scallops with tomatoes and garlic, 53
  Seafood salad, hot, 59
  Shrimp Greek style, 58
  Shrimp and mushrooms in phyllo, 56
  Shrimp, Neptune's favorite, 54
  Shrimp and sole mousse in cabbage, 4
  Sole Alma, 34
  Sole, fillets of, mushroomed, 38
  Sole mousse with sherry sauce, 36
  Sole, rex in red wine, 40
  Trout baked with sour cream, 45
  Trout cornmealed, 50
  Trout filled with halibut mousse, 46
  Trout "in the manner of" La Pyramide, 48
  Tunafish and bean appetizer, 25
  Whitefish, smoked with avocado, 26
  Whitefish with sweet peppers, 39

Four vegetables with cheese sauce, 126
French crusty rye bread, 158
French fried potato baskets, 135
French lemon tart, 201
Fresh peach tart, 202
Frozen Grand Marnier bonbons, 227
Frozen orange delicious, 241
Fruited rice, 122

Game hens
   With noodles and raisins, 86
   With picadillo, 84
   With rice-waterchestnut stuffing, 84
Garlic oil, 28
Genoise, 185
   Cassata alla siciliana, 228
   With raspberries and whipped cream, 233
Ginger
   Asparagus, a Chinese way, 125
   Dressing, for chicken salad, 149
   Ice cream, 246
Goose, with apple and prune stuffing, 83
Gougère, 117
Grand finale chocolate gâteau, 178
Grand Marnier
   Cassata alla siciliana, 228
   Chocolate-orange pots de crème, 223
   Frozen bonbons, 227
   Frozen soufflés, 235
   Grand finale chocolate gâteau, 178
   Ice cream, 244
Grapefruit sorbet, 237
Grapes
   Chicken breasts with, 76
   And fennel salad, 144
Greek salad with fennel and feta, 145
Green beans, four vegetables with cheese sauce, 126
Green chiles, see Chiles
Green corn tamales, 116
Green goddess
   Dressing, 150
   Seafood salad, 150
Green mayonnaise, 154
Green peppers, see Peppers
Green sauce
   For Mexican chicken, 68
   For Mexican pork, 101
Guacamole, 42

Gumbo (Crab, shrimp, and oyster), 60

Haddock mousse, Anna's smoked, 20
Halibut mousse, 46
Ham
   Crêpe appetizer gâteau, 23
   Russian buffet salad, 151
   Seafood salad, hot, 59
   Two canapé cakes, 18
Hearts of boston lettuce with egg dressing, 144
Heavenly brioche, 161
Herring with apple, onion, and dill, 14
Honey-walnut rolls, 162
Hors d'oeuvres, see Appetizers and First Courses
Horseradish sauce, 92
Hot seafood salad, 59

Ice cream
   Cinnamon, 243
   Coffee, 242
   Fresh pineapple and rum, 246
   Fresh strawberry, 245
   Ginger, 246
   Grand Marnier, 244
   Peach, 244
   Praline, 245
   Rich dark chocolate, 242
   Rum, chestnut, and cherry, 247
   Vanilla, 241
   See also Sorbet
Icings
   Chocolate (Ganache), 187
   For cinnamon rolls, 164
   For walnut coffeecake, 166
   Lemon, 173
   Strawberry, fresh, 183
Indonesian lamb roasts with peaches and chutney, 93

Jack cheese
   Chicken enchiladas, 114
   Crabmeat enchiladas, 112
   Green corn tamales, 116

Lamb
   Chops, baked, 96
   Indonesian lamb roasts with peaches and chutney, 94

Leg of, with potatoes and onions, 95
Racks of, 96
Stew, 97
Lasagne rolls, 110
Lemons
  Cake, 173
  French tart, 201
  Icing, 173
  Sauce, 218
  Sorbet, 237
Lettuce
  Boston, hearts of with egg dressing, 144
  Cobb salad, 143
  See also Romaine
Liver, see Chicken livers
Lobster
  Avocados filled with, 17
  Tails with butter and lemon, 52
  With waterchestnuts, 51

Macadamia nuts
  Chicken salad in cantaloupe, 149
  Pineapple-rum cake, 182
Macaroons
  Almond, 189
  Strawberry cake, 184
Madeira sauce, 90
Majestic chicken, 74
Mandelbrodt, 195
Mandelschnitten, 196
Marinades
  For antipasto, 12
  For Indonesian lamb roasts, 94
  Teriyaki, 104
Mayonnaise, green, 154
Medley of white corn and celery, 128
Melon
  Honeydew, avocado, and tomato salad, 141
  See also Cantaloupe
Meringue, filbert circles, 230
Meringue shells, 247
  With chocolate sauce and walnut praline, 216
  With fresh oranges and caramel-orange sauce, 215
Mexican chicken with green sauce, 68
Mexican pork in green sauce, 101

Monte Alban chicken en papillote, 66
Mornay sauce, 79
Mousses
  Halibut, 46
  Shrimp and sole in cabbage, 4
  Sole with sherry sauce, 36
Mushrooms
  Duxelles, 72
  Filling for sole Alma, 34
  Filling for steak in crêpes, 90
  And phyllo pastries, 10
  Sauce, 74
  Sauce for sole, 38
  Sauce for spinach roll, 118
  Seafood salad, hot, 59
  And shrimp in phyllo, 56
  Tartlets, 11
Mustard
  Sauce, 102
  And sour cream sauce, 26

Noodles and raisin stuffing, 86
Nuts
  Danish pastry pecan rolls, 168
  Peanuts, with Mexican pork in green sauce, 101
  Pine nuts with wild rice and currants, 121
  Tiny chocolate délices, with pistachio nuts, 188
  See also Almonds, Filberts, Macadamia nuts, Walnuts

Old-fashioned fried chicken, 67
Onions
  Alsatian onion pie, 3
  With herring, apple, and dill, 14
  With leg of lamb, 95
  With potatoes and cheese, 136
  Red, and pickled beets salad, 142
  Red cabbage and raisin slaw, 141
Oranges
  Chocolate filling, 178
  Frozen delicious, 241
  With meringues and caramel-orange sauce, 215
  Sauce for ducklings, 82
  Sorbet, 238
  And spinach salad, 148
Oysters, crab, and shrimp gumbo, 60

Pancakes, potato, 134; *see also* Crêpes
Papaya, Chicken in, 69
Papillotes
  Monte Alban chicken in, 66
  Salmon in, 31
Paradisaical hot apple tarts, 199
Parmesan cheese
  Fettucine Alfredo-Mellinkoff, 109
  Filling for lasagne rolls, 110
  Shrimp and mushrooms in phyllo, 56
Pasta
  Fettucine Alfredo-Mellinkoff, 109
  Lasagne rolls, 110
  Spaghetti carbonara, 107
  Spaghetti springtime, 108
Pastries
  Apple dumplings, 200
  Apple tarts, 199
  Blue plum tart, 203
  Caramel-walnut tart with chocolate glaze, 206
  Congress tarts, 205
  Danish pastry pecan rolls, 168
  French lemon tart, 201
  Fresh peach tart, 202
  Mushroom-phyllo, 10
  Mushroom tartlets, 11
  Phyllo cheese, in a Rumanian mode, 204
  Puff pastry, asparagus in, 8
  See also Phyllo, Puff pastry, Pastry
Pastry
  Apricot bars, base for, 192
  Mandelschnitten, base for, 196
  Puff, 211
  Rich, 210
  Sweet, 210
Pastry cream favorite, 248
Pâtés
  Chicken liver mousse, 15
  Chicken liver pâté with port wine aspic, 16
  Haddock mousse, 20
  Salmon and sole, 13
Peaches
  With ducklings, 81
  Fresh tart, 202
  Ice cream, 244
  With Indonesian lamb roasts, 94
  Sorbet, 238
Pears
  Avocado Fontainebleau, 26
  Sorbet, 239
Pepper, green
  Chicken "country captain" style, 70
  Combination salad, 145
  With cream, 129
  Greek salad with fennel and feta, 145
Peppers, red
  Cantaloupe and romaine salad, 142
  With green and yellow peppers, 130
  With green for whitefish, 39
Perfectly easy racks of lamb, 96
Phyllo
  Boned chicken breasts in, 72
  Cheese pastries in a Rumanian mode, 204
  Mushroom-phyllo pastries, 10
  Shrimp and mushrooms in, 56
  Spinach strudel, 132
Pickled beets and red onion salad, 142
Pies, *see* Pastries and Pastry
Pike, baked with vegetables and red wine, 44
Pimento-anchovy canapés, 14
Pineapple
  With ducklings, 80
  Macadamia-rum cake, 182
  Rum ice cream, 246
Plums, blue plum tart, 203
Pomegranates
  Chiles en nogada, 24
  Roasted chicken pomegranate, 63
Popovers, 163
Pork
  Chiles en nogada, 24
  Chops, stuffed, and with mustard sauce, 102
  Mexican, in green sauce, 101
  Picadillo stuffing, 24
  Sausage, in cornbread stuffing, 78
  Spareribs teriyaki, 104
  See also Bacon
Potatoes
  Anna, in nonstick skillets, 133
  Baskets, french fried, 135
  Pancakes, 134
  With onions and cheese, 136
Praline
  Ice cream, 245

In caramel lace baskets, 232
Paste, 248
Walnut, 216
Prunes and apple stuffing, 83
Puff pastry, 211
   Apple tarts, 199
   Asparagus in, 8
   Raspberries with caramel sauce, 208

Rack of veal madeira, 98
Raisins
   Chicken "country captain" style, 70
   Cinnamon rolls, 164
   Fruited rice, 122
   Noodle stuffing for game hens, 86
   Picadillo, 24
   Red cabbage and onion slaw, 141
   Walnut filling for crêpes with chocolate sauce, 226
Raspberries
   On genoise with whipped cream, 233
   On leaves, 234
   On puff pastry with caramel sauce, 208
   Sorbet, 239
Red cabbage, raisin, and onion slaw, 141
Rice
   Fruited, 122
   Waterchestnut stuffing, 84
   Wild, with pine nuts and currants, 121
   Wild, stuffing, 77
Rich dark chocolate ice cream, 242
Rich pastry, 210
Ricotta cheese
   Cassata alla siciliana, 228
   Filling, lasagne rolls, 104
Rolls
   Butter, 160
   Cinnamon, family-style, 164
   Crisp water, 157
   Danish pastry pecan, 168
   Brioche, 161
   Honey-walnut, 162
Romaine
   Bean sprout salad, 146
   Cantaloupe and red pepper salad, 142
   Spinach and almond salad, 147
Roquefort cheese (Cobb salad), 143
Rum
   Chestnut and cherry ice cream, 247

Macadamia-pineapple cake, 182
Pineapple ice cream, 246
Walnut filling for crêpes, 226
Rumaki with watermelon pickles, 6
Russian buffet salad, 151
Russian dressing, 153
Rye bread, French crusty, 158

Salad dressings
   Egg, 144
   Ginger, for chicken in cantaloupe, 149
   Green goddess, 150
   Green mayonnaise, 154
   Russian, 153
   Sour cream-dill, 153
   For spinach and orange salad, 148
   For spinach, romaine, and almond salad, 147
   Vinaigrette, 152
Salads
   Avocado, tomato, and honeydew melon, 141
   Cantaloupe, red pepper, and romaine, 142
   Chicken in cantaloupe, 149
   Cobb, 143
   Combination, 145
   Fennel and green grape, 144
   Greek salad with fennel and feta, 145
   Hearts of boston lettuce with egg dressing, 144
   Pickled beets and red onion, 142
   Red cabbage, raisin, and onion slaw, 141
   Romaine and bean sprout, 146
   Russian buffet, 151
   Seafood, 150
   Spinach and orange, 148
   Spinach, romaine, and almond, 147
Salami (crêpe appetizer gâteau), 23
Salmon
   And sole pâté, 13
   In papillote, 31
   Steaks in foil packets, 33
Sauces
   For antipasto, 12
   Apricot, 200
   For asparagus in puff pastry, 8
   Caramel, 208
   Caramel-orange, 215

Champagne, for salmon, 32
Cheddar cheese, 126
For chicken enchiladas, 114
Chocolate, 216, 236
For crabmeat enchiladas, 112
Cream cheese and walnut, 24
Dill-watercress, 54
For ducklings, 81
Green, for Mexican chicken, 68
Green, for Mexican pork, 101
Horseradish, 92
Lemon, 218
For lobster with waterchestnuts, 51
Madeira, 90
Monte Alban, 66
Mornay, 79
Mushroom, for chicken, 74
Mushroom, for sole, 38
Mushroom, for spinach roll, 118
Mustard, 102
Orange for ducklings, 82
Shallot butter, 4
Sherry, for sole mousse, 36
Sole Alma, 34
Sour cream-mustard, 26
Spicy, for beef tenderloins, 89
Teriyaki, 104
Tomato, for green corn tamales, 116
Tomato, for lasagne rolls, 110
Tomato, for shrimp Greek style, 58
For trout filled with halibut mousse, 46
Watercress, 26
Whipped butter, 40
Scallops, with tomatoes and garlic, 53
Sesame seeds
   Spinach and orange salad, 148
   Wing-drumsticks, 7
Shallot butter sauce, 4
Shellfish, *see* Fish and Seafood; Crab; etc.
Shrimp
   Crab and oyster gumbo, 60
   Greek style, 58
   And mushrooms in phyllo, 56
   Neptune's favorite, 54
   Russian buffet salad, 151
   Seafood salad, hot, 59
   And sole mousse in cabbage, 4
Simply baked corn, 129

Smoked turkey omelet, 120
Sole
   Alma, 34
   Fillets of, mushroomed, 38
   Mousse and shrimp in cabbage, 4
   Mousse with sherry sauce, 36
   Rex in red wine, 40
   And salmon pâté, 13
Soufflé, Grand Marnier frozen, 235
Sorbet
   Grapefruit, 237
   Lemon, 237
   Orange, 238
   Peach, 238
   Pear, 239
   Raspberry, 239
   Strawberry, 240
   Watermelon, 240
Sour cream
   Dill dressing, 153
   Mustard sauce, 26
   Trout baked with, 45
Spaghetti
   Carbonara, 107
   Springtime, 108
Spareribs teriyaki, 104
Spinach
   Crêpe appetizer gâteau, 23
   Filling for lasagne rolls, 110
   And orange salad, 148
   Phyllo strudel, 132
   Quiche, Greek style, 131
   Roll with scrambled eggs, 118
   Romaine and almond salad, 147
   Turkey mornay on, 79
   Zucchini stuffed with, 137
Sponge cake with fresh strawberry icing, 183
Springtime spaghetti, 108
Stan and Don's chicken in papaya, 69
Steak in crêpes with madeira sauce, 90
Stocks
   Court bouillon, 42
   Fish, 46, 48
Strawberries
   Ice cream, 245
   Icing, 183
   Macaroon cake, 184
   On leaves, 234
   Sorbet, 240

Stuffed pork chops with mustard sauce, 102
Stuffings
  Apple and prune, 83
  Cornbread, 78
  For chicken breasts, 74
  Noodles and raisins, 86
  Picadillo, 24
  For pork chops, 102
  Rice-waterchestnut, 84
  Vegetable, for trout, 48
  Wild rice, 77
Sweet pastry, 210

Tamales, green corn, 116
Teriyaki sauce, 104
Tiny chocolate délices, 188
Tomatoes
  Avocado and honeydew melon salad, 141
  Cobb salad, 143
  Combination salad, 145
  Greek salad with fennel and feta, 145
  Romaine and bean sprout salad, 146
  Sauce for green corn tamales, 116
  Sauce for lasagne rolls, 110
  Sauce, shrimp Greek style, 58
  Two canapé cakes, 18
Tortillas
  Beef burritos, 115
  Chicken enchiladas, 114
  Crabmeat enchiladas, 112
Trout
  Baked with sour cream, 45
  Cornmealed, 50
  Filled with halibut mousse, 46
  "In the manner of" La Pyramide, 48
Tuiles, 193
Tunafish
  Antipasto, 12
  And bean appetizer, 25
Turkey
  With cornbread stuffing, 78
  Mornay, on spinach, 79
  Smoked, omelet, 120
  With wild rice stuffing, 77
Tuscan bean and tunafish appetizer, 25
Twenty-four chicken enchiladas, 114
Two canapé cakes, 18

Vanilla ice cream, 241
  With brandied cherries and chocolate sauce, 236
  With meringues, chocolate sauce, and walnut praline, 216
  With meringues, fresh oranges, and caramel-orange sauce, 215
Veal
  Chops, Italian style, 99
  Chops, marsala, 100
  Rack of, madeira, 98
Vegetables
  Alsatian onion pie, 3
  Asparagus, a Chinese way, 125
  Asparagus in puff pastry, 8
  Big party antipasto, 12
  Carrots and celery, 128
  Corn, simply baked, 129
  Four vegetables with cheese sauce, 126
  Green peppers with cream, 129
  Green, red, and yellow sweet peppers, 130
  Medley of white corn and celery, 128
  Mushroom-phyllo pastries, 10
  Mushroom tartlets, 10
  Okra, in crab, shrimp, and oyster gumbo, 60
  Pike baked with vegetables and red wine, 44
  Potato baskets, french fried, 135
  Potato pancakes, 134
  Potatoes Anna in nonstick skillets, 133
  Potatoes, onions, and cheese, 136
  Red cabbage, braised, 127
  Russian buffet salad, 151
  Spinach, in crêpe appetizer gâteau, 23
  Spinach phyllo strudel, 132
  Spinach quiche, Greek style, 131
  Spinach roll with scrambled eggs, 118
  Springtime spaghetti, 108
  Stuffing for trout, 48
  Zucchini stuffed with spinach, 137
  See also Appetizers and First Courses; Salads; names of vegetables
Vinaigrette, 152

Walnuts
  And cream cheese sauce, 24
  Caramel tart with chocolate glaze, 206

Coffeecake, 166
Filling for crêpes with chocolate sauce, 226
Honey-walnut rolls, 162
Praline, 216
Waterchestnuts
　Lobster with, 51
　Rice stuffing, 84
　Shrimp and mushrooms in phyllo, 56
Watercress
　Dill-watercress sauce, 54
　Sauce, 26

Springtime spaghetti, 108
Watermelon sorbet, 240
Waterzooï chicken, 64
Whipped butter sauce, 40
Whitefish
　With sweet peppers, 39
　Smoked, avocado Fontainebleau, 26
Whole poached fish with guacamole, 42
Wing-drumsticks with sesame seeds, 7

Zucchini stuffed with spinach, 137